Quick Guide

POOL & SPA MAINTENANCE

[Cronin, John]

CREATIVE HOMEOWNER PRESS®

COPYRIGHT © 1998, 1996
CREATIVE HOMEOWNER PRESS®
A Division of Federal Marketing Corp.
Upper Saddle River, NJ

Manufactured in the United States of America

Editorial Director: Timothy O. Bakke
Art Director: Annie Jeon

Writer: John Cronin
Technical Consultant: Terry Tamminen
Editor: Alexander Samuelson
Editorial Assistant: Patrick Quinn
Copy Editor: Kimberly Catanzarite

Graphic Designers: Michelle D. Halko
                   Michael J. Allegra
Illustrators: Jon Rasula
              Jim Randolph
              Paul M. Schumm
              Craig M. Franklin

Cover Design: Warren Ramezzana
Cover Illustrations: Paul M. Schumm

Electronic Prepress and Printing:
Command Web Offset, Inc.

Current Printing (last digit)
10 9 8 7 6 5 4 3 2

Quick Guide: Pool & Spa Maintenance
Library of Congress Catalog Card Number: 94-69653
ISBN: 1-880029-43-X (paper)

CREATIVE HOMEOWNER PRESS®
A Division of Federal Marketing Corp.
24 Park Way
Upper Saddle River, NJ 07458

C O N T E N T S

S A F E T Y   F I R S T

Though all the designs and methods in this book have been tested for safety, it is not possible to overstate the importance of using the safest construction methods possible. What follows are reminders; some do's and don'ts for repair and maintenance. They are not substitutes for your own common sense.

■ *Always* use caution, care, and good judgment when following the procedures described in this book.

■ *Always* be sure that the electrical setup is safe. Be sure that no circuit is overloaded, that all power tools and electrical outlets are properly grounded, and that electrical outlets in damp or wet locations are protected by a ground-fault circuit interruptor (GFCI). Do not use power tools in wet locations.

■ *Always* read container labels on paints, solvents, and other products; provide ventilation, and observe all other warnings.

■ *Always* read the tool manufacturer's instructions for using a tool, especially the warnings.

■ *Always* store pool chemicals and supplies in a locked, well ventilated area.

■ *Always* pay deliberate attention to how a tool works so that you can avoid being injured.

■ *Always* know the limitations of your tools. Do not try to force them to do what they were not designed to do.

■ *Always* be aware of the end of the deck when working near the pool.

■ *Always* wear the appropriate rubber or work gloves and eye protection when handling any pool chemicals.

■ *Always* keep your hands away from the business ends of blades, cutters, and bits.

■ *Always* wear a disposable face mask when you create dust by sawing or sanding. Use a special filtering respirator when working with toxic substances and solvents.

■ *Always* wear eye protection, especially when using power tools or striking metal on metal or concrete; a chip can fly off, for example, when chiseling concrete.

■ *Always* be aware that there is seldom time for your body's reflexes to save you from injury from a power tool in a dangerous situation; everything happens too fast. Be *alert!*

■ *Always* check your local building codes when adding a diving board. The codes are intended to protect public safety and should be observed to the letter.

■ *Never* work with power tools when you are tired or under the influence of alcohol or drugs.

■ *Never* cut tiny pieces of wood or pipe using a power saw. Cut small pieces off larger pieces.

■ *Never* change a saw blade or a drill or router bit unless the power cord is unplugged. Do not depend on the switch being off; you might accidentally hit it.

■ *Never* work in insufficient lighting.

■ *Never* mix acid and chlorine. The combination creates a deadly chlorine gas.

■ *Never* carry sharp or pointed tools, such as utility knives, awls, or chisels in your pocket. If you want to carry tools, use a special-purpose tool belt with leather pockets and holders.

■ *Never* add trichlor to a vinyl or dark-colored plaster-top-coated pool. The concentration of chemicals weakens the vinyl and bleaches out the color.

■ *Never* add a granular product directly to a pool skimmer.

■ *Never* operate a booster pump system unless the circulation pump is working as well.

■ *Never* turn on a pool light unless there is water in the pool. The light fixture is watertight and the air inside of it becomes extremely hot.

■ *Never* drain all the water out of an in-ground pool or spa because hydrostatic pressure can cause cracks, or worse, it can cause the pool to pop out of the ground.

■ *Never* get chlorine on your skin or in your eyes. Use water to flush your eyes if splashed with chlorine.

POOL MAINTENANCE TOOLS & SUPPLIES

Specific tools and equipment are necessary for the maintenance, cleaning, and general upkeep of spas and pools. In addition, there are several chemicals needed to maintain a body of clean, healthy water.

Tools for Maintenance & Repair

Below is a collection of basic tools needed for the procedures in this book. While it is not important for you to be a plumber, electrician, mason, or carpenter, it is important to know that a working pool, and its related equipment, often encompasses all of these trades. The right tool for the job can make the difference between getting something done correctly and creating new, more drastic problems. The specialty tools, cleaning equipment, and chemicals listed here are described in detail later in the book.

Basic Tools

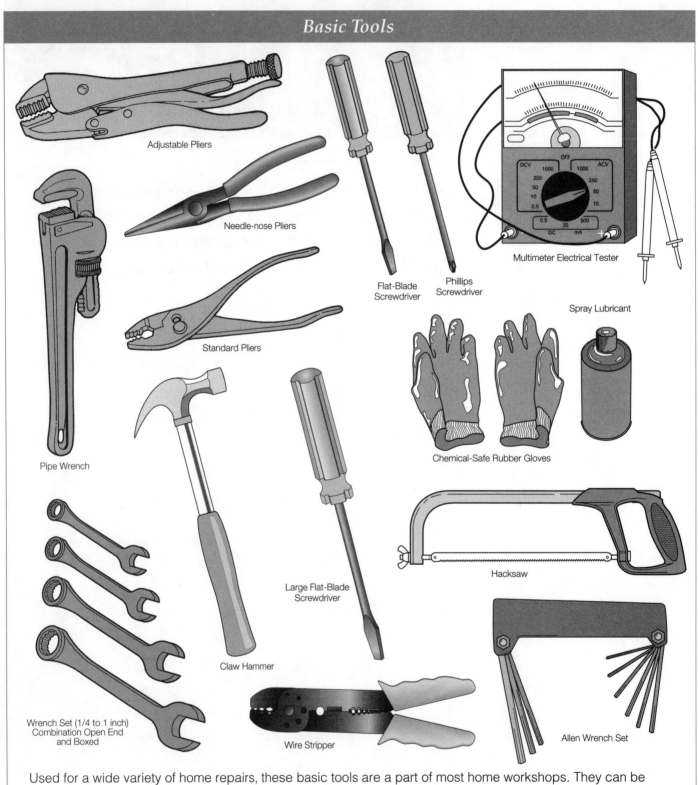

Adjustable Pliers

Needle-nose Pliers

Pipe Wrench

Standard Pliers

Flat-Blade Screwdriver

Phillips Screwdriver

Multimeter Electrical Tester

Spray Lubricant

Chemical-Safe Rubber Gloves

Claw Hammer

Large Flat-Blade Screwdriver

Hacksaw

Wrench Set (1/4 to 1 inch) Combination Open End and Boxed

Wire Stripper

Allen Wrench Set

Used for a wide variety of home repairs, these basic tools are a part of most home workshops. They can be purchased at home centers and hardware stores.

Special Pool Tools

In addition to the common tools already mentioned, some tools and equipment that are specially designed for pool maintenance and repair are necessary. Pool tools, equipment, and chemicals are available at pool supply stores.

Telepole. The most important cleaning tool is an 8-foot telepole that extends (telescopes) to 16 feet. One end of the pole has a grip or a rounded tip that prevents your hand from slipping. Some telepoles have a magnetic tip for picking up metal found on the bottom of the pool. Telepoles are made of aluminum or fiberglass. Fiberglass poles are worth the slightly higher cost because they do not corrode, they are very sturdy, and they do not conduct electricity should they come in contact with exposed wires. Also available are 4- and 12-foot telepoles that extend to twice their length.

Many of the tools described below have handles that fit inside the end of the telepole and clip in place by means of a tool clip.

Leaf Rakes. These tools have an aluminum frame with a plastic or stainless-steel mesh net. While more expensive than leaf rakes, deep-net leaf rakes allow cleaning at greater depths. The aluminum rakes are covered with a plastic gasket to withstand rubbing along rough plaster surfaces. The shank of the rake fits into the end of the telepole and a tool clip locks it in place. Do not spill caustic chemicals on the leaf rake. Some rakes are designed so the netting can be replaced.

Wall Brush. The wall brush is either straight or curved (at the ends only) and has nylon or stainless steel bristles. The curved brush is better at getting into pool corners and step areas. The most common brush is 18 inches wide. A 6-inch brush is better for spas. Always use a stainless-steel wire brush for stubborn stains

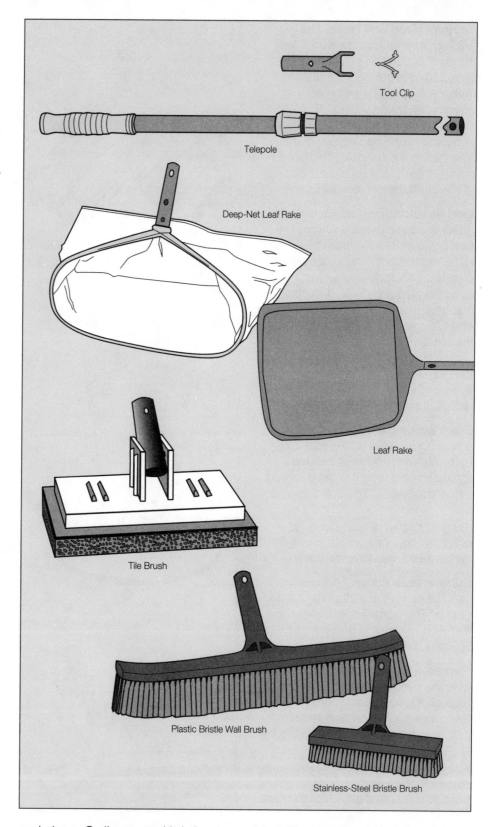

Tool Clip

Telepole

Deep-Net Leaf Rake

Leaf Rake

Tile Brush

Plastic Bristle Wall Brush

Stainless-Steel Bristle Brush

and algae. Ordinary steel bristles break off and stain the plaster when they rust.

Tile Brush. These brushes are about 6 inches long and have an abrasive foam pad or plastic bristles for scrub-

bing. They are handy for wiping algae off ladders or spots in a spa. An extension pole makes the task of scrubbing easier, although brushes can be used by themselves.

Vacuum Head and Hose. The vacuum head and hose works with the pool circulation equipment. The hose (10–50-foot lengths) attaches to the bottom of the skimmer opening to create suction. The other end of the hose connects to the vacuum head. The vacuum head attaches to the telepole. The head is made of flexible plastic, so it curves to the contours of the pool bottom.

Leaf Vacuum. The leaf vacuum attaches to the telepole and operates by forcing water from a garden hose into the unit. The water is then diverted into dozens of tiny jets directed (upward) toward a fabric leaf bag. The upwelling water creates a vacuum at the base of the plastic helmet, sucking leaves and debris into the unit and into the bag. As the water passes through the mesh of the bag, the debris is trapped.

Spa Vacuum. The spa vacuum is a miniature version of the leaf vacuum. Water pressure is created by a garden hose and the dirt is forced into a small sock. The spa vacuum attaches to the telepole and has many of its own attachments for reaching crevices and brushing the surface as it vacuums.

Submersible Pump. This device is used to pump the water out of a pool or spa. The pump recirculates the last inch of water to prevent running dry and burning out.

Pumice Stones. Made from volcanic ash, the pumice stone is abrasive enough to remove scale from tiles and other stains and deposits from plaster without scratching excessively. Pumice stones are sold as brick-sized blocks, or as small blade stones that attach to a telepole for hard to reach places. Try both types. Since they disintegrate, it is smart to use them before vacuuming.

Blow Bag. (2-Inch Drain Flush.) Made of canvas or rubber, a blow bag is used to prime a pump. One end attaches to a garden hose and the other goes into the skimmer hole

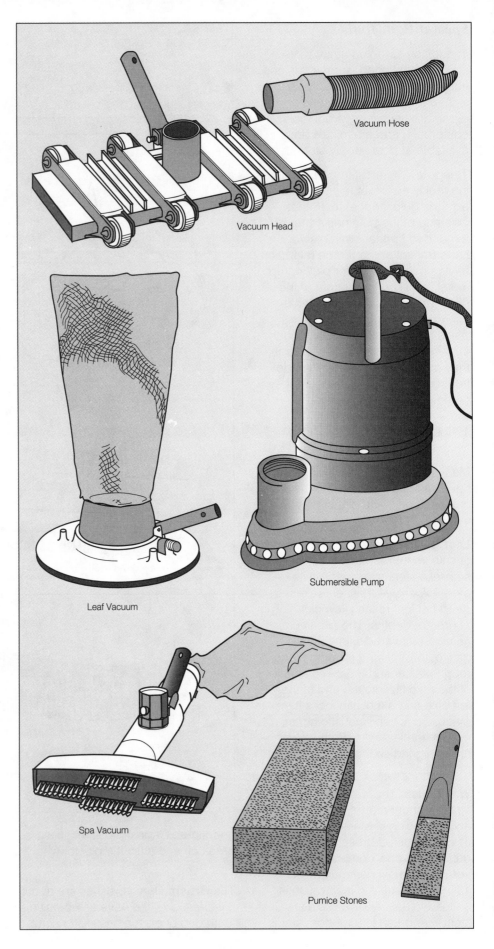

Vacuum Hose

Vacuum Head

Leaf Vacuum

Submersible Pump

Spa Vacuum

Pumice Stones

that feeds the pump. When filled with water the bag expands and seals the skimmer hole so water is fed from the hose into the pump. The injection of water primes the pump. The blow bag does not work on skimmers that have only one hole in the bottom connecting it to the pump and the main drain.

Test Kit. A test kit contains the chemical reagents necessary to run tests for various water chemistry levels.

Pool Chemicals. Proper pool maintenance requires several chemicals including a sanitizer such as chlorine, an acid for lowering pH levels, and soda ash for raising pH levels. (See chapter 2, "Water Chemistry," page 11.)

Air Pump. When you close a pool in cold climates you need a small air pump to pressurize the return lines before plugging them for the winter.

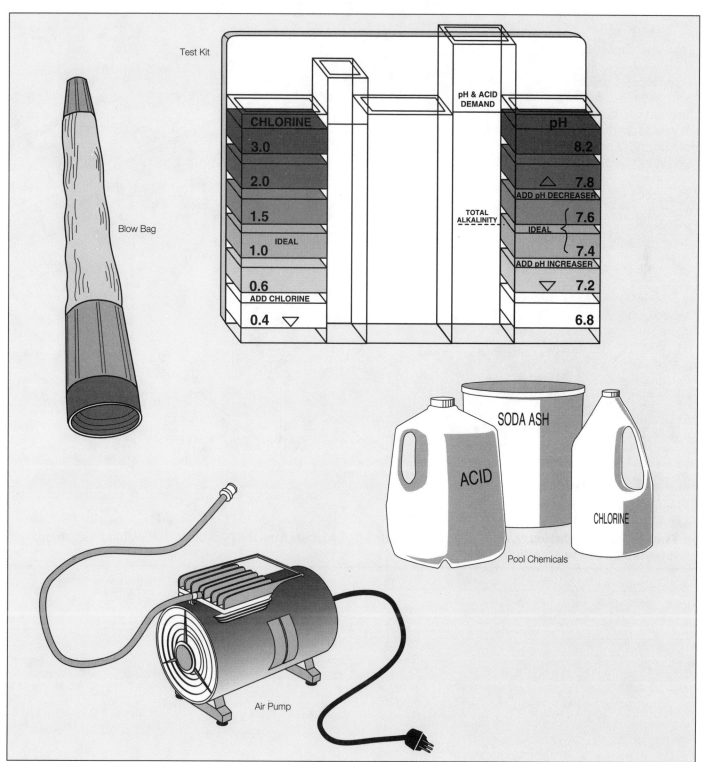

Test Kit

Blow Bag

CHLORINE
3.0
2.0
1.5
1.0   IDEAL
0.6
ADD CHLORINE
0.4 ▽

pH & ACID DEMAND

TOTAL ALKALINITY

pH
8.2
△ 7.8
ADD pH DECREASER
7.6
IDEAL
7.4
ADD pH INCREASER
▽ 7.2
6.8

SODA ASH

ACID

CHLORINE

Pool Chemicals

Air Pump

Pool & Spa Circulation System

Repairing and maintaining a pool or spa is not difficult once you understand basically how the water and equipment work together. Pools and spas, simply put, are large containers of circulating water. Like any closed circulation system, be it human blood or gasoline through an engine, the water takes a logical route as it travels from the pool through the plumbing, pump, filter, heater, and back again.

Water begins its trip at the skimmer or the main drain. A motor-driven pump provides the suction that gets the water moving. After shooting through the pump, the water is cleaned by a filter, pushed through the heater's coils (if there is a heater), and returned to the pool or spa through the return ports.

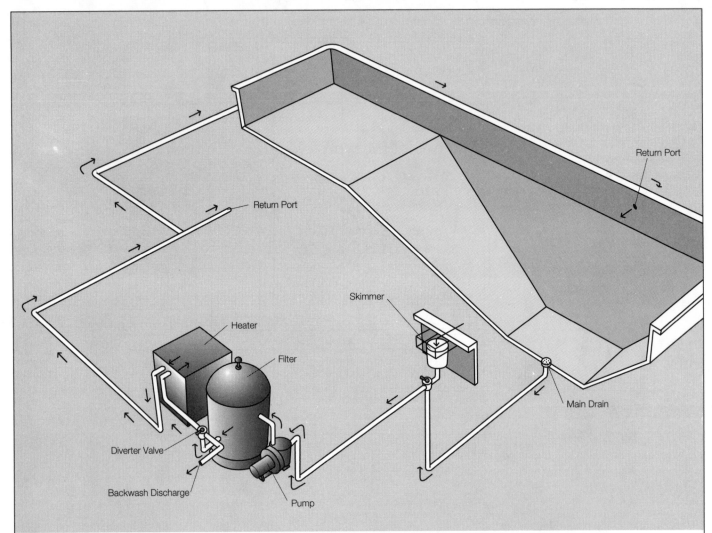

Pool & Spa Circulation System. The water travels a logical route from the pool through the plumbing, pump, filter, heater, and back again.

WATER CHEMISTRY

Do not let the word chemistry frighten you. There are simple concepts and approaches that demystify the subject of water chemistry and keep your pool and spa sparkling and clean.

Estimating Water Volume

The volume of water in a pool or spa dictates the amount of chemicals required. Therefore, the first step is to calculate the volume.

Round off each measurement to the nearest foot or percentage of a foot. One inch equals 0.0833 foot, so multiply the number of inches measured by 0.0833 to get the percentage of one foot.

Example: 29 ft. 9 in. =
29 ft. + (9 in. X 0.0833) =
29 + 0.75 = 29.75 ft.

The average depth can be estimated. For example, if the shallow end is 3 feet and the deep end is 9 feet, the average depth lies halfway between the two, at 6 feet.

When calculating the average depth, be sure to use actual water depth rather than the depth of the pool or spa itself. In the example, the spa is 4 feet deep, but the water is only filled to approximately 3 feet. If 4 feet is used for calculations, it results in a volume that is 33 percent higher than the actual amount. Because chemicals are administered according to water volume, a mistake like this can cause serious problems.

Square or Rectangular. Use the following formula to figure the volume of a square or rectangular pool or spa:

Length x Width x
Average Depth x 7.5 =
Volume (in gallons)

Length times width equals the surface area of the pool. Multiply this answer by the average depth to come up with the volume in cubic feet. Lastly, there are 7.5 gallons of water in each cubic foot, so multiply the number of cubic feet by 7.5. This yields the volume of the pool in gallons.

Circular. The formula for determining the volume of a circular pool is as follows:

3.14 x Radius Squared x
Average Depth x 7.5 =
Volume (in gallons)

The radius is one-half the diameter, so measure the distance across the broadest part of the pool and divide that number in half. Multiply the radius times itself (square it). For example, if the radius is 5 feet, multiply 5 feet x 5 feet to get 25 feet. Then multiply the radius squared by 3.14. The rest of the formula is the same as the square or rectangular equation.

Spas. Because of the built-in seats, an empty circular spa looks like an

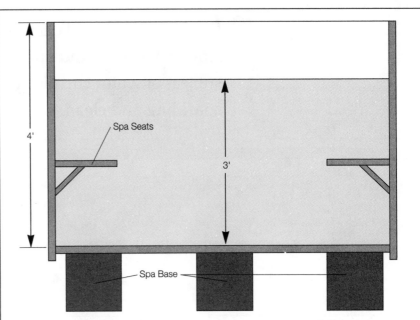

Estimating Water Volume. Use the actual water depth, not the depth of the pool or spa itself.

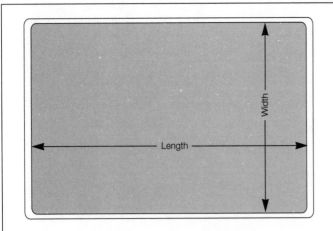

Square or Rectangle. Area = Length x Width.
Volume (in gallons) = Area x Average Depth x 7.5

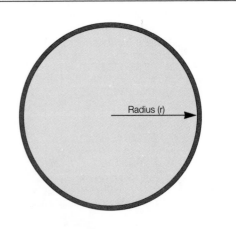

Circular. Area = 3.14 x r².
Volume (in gallons) = Area x Average depth x 7.5

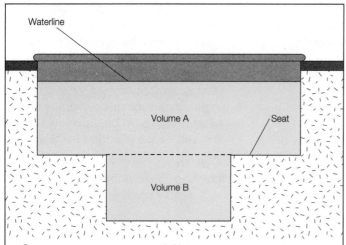

Spas. Treat spas as two different volumes: volume A above the seats to the waterline and volume B below the seats.

Kidney or Odd Shapes. Break down the pool into a combination of smaller regular shapes.

upside-down wedding cake. When calculating volume, break the spa into two different volumes: volume A above the seats to the waterline; and volume B below the seats. A wooden hot tub is measured as if there are no seats because there is water above and below them, making the difference negligible.

Kidney or Odd Shapes. Break down the pool into a combination of smaller regular shapes. Use the formulas already described for each square, rectangular, or circular area. Add the volumes together for total capacity.

Components of Healthy Water

Few pools achieve a perfect water balance at all times, but the following are excellent parameters to shoot for:

Chlorine Residual	1.0-3.0 ppm
Total Alkalinity	80-150 ppm
pH	7.4-7.6
Hardness	200-400 ppm
Total Dissolved Solids (TDS)	Less than 2000 ppm
Cyanuric Acid	30-80 ppm

ppm=parts per million

Water chemistry is a process of balance dictated by a demand for

what is missing. Whenever something is added to a pool, the balance of everything else is affected. This is why it is important to learn about each component and how to achieve optimum conditions for each. Before pouring chemicals into the pool or spa, consider the consequences of everything that is done (or not done).

Chlorine Residual

The chlorine residual is the amount of sanitizing chlorine available in the

water. Sanitizers such as chlorine kill bacteria in water. Bacteria stimulate algae growth and carry disease. There are other sanitizing methods, and many other products on the market that kill special algae and get rid of stains, but chlorine remains the benchmark. Chlorine is available in liquid, dry tablet, or granular form.

Liquid Chlorine. Liquid sanitizer has a very low pH. When adding liquid chlorine, this fact must be considered. Since it already is a

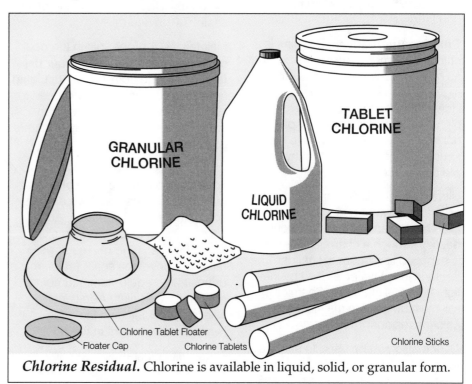

Chlorine Residual. Chlorine is available in liquid, solid, or granular form.

liquid, the advantage of liquid chlorine is that it goes into solution immediately. Chlorine bleaches everything it comes in contact with, so to prevent splashes, pour liquid chlorine close to the surface of the water. This also ensures that the proper strength goes into the pool.

Dry Chlorine. Dry chlorine is available in granular or tablet form and may or may not contain cyanurates. Cyanurates act as a stabilizer, helping to prevent the chlorine from breaking down.

Calcium hypochlorite (often called "cal-hypo") is dry chlorine that does not contain cyanurates. It comes in tablet or granular form and often is used as a shocking agent (see page 16).

Dry chlorine with stabilizing cyanurates is called either dichlor or trichlor. Dichlor is 56 to 63 percent available chlorine and does not leave a sediment. Trichlor is the most concentrated form of chlorine produced and dissolves slowly in a floater. It is very acidic. Granular trichlor is produced as a super killing agent for algae blooms. It can dissolve metal, so make sure that the floater or dispenser is kept away from anything made of metal including the skimmer, rails, and ladders.

Chlorine Alternatives. Bromine is a chlorine alternative, but it is not used as much as chlorine because it is highly unstable and is expensive. However, bromine works well at the high temperatures found in spas and hot tubs, and it does not have the strong chlorine odor that many people do not like.

Ultraviolet light (UV) is another sanitizer. After the water passes the pump, filter, heater, and other equipment, it passes through a chamber where it is exposed to a beam of UV light. The bacteria in the water is killed by the light from this chamber. Chemicals still must be used to maintain a chlorine residual in the water.

Ozone also can be used to sanitize pool water. Water circulates through an ozone generator where oxygen bubbles are pumped into the water. Ozone is very unstable, but it does have some residual sanitizing properties. Like UV light, it cannot be used alone but requires booster chemicals to clean thoroughly.

Total Alkalinity

Total alkalinity is the quantity of alkaline material in the water. Do not confuse total alkalinity with pH or hardness. Total alkalinity has an impact on pH and hardness, but it is not the same thing. It is a measurement of the soluble minerals in the water. The total alkalinity of a pool is acceptable when it falls between 80 and 150 parts per million. Total alkalinity is raised by adding baking soda or soda ash; it is lowered by adding muriatic acid. Always adjust the total alkalinity level first and pH second. By maintaining the total alkalinity, the pool uses less acid and less chlorine and has fewer algae problems.

pH Levels

pH readings are a way to estimate the relative alkalinity or acidity of water. The pH scale ranges from 0 to 14. 0 is extremely acidic and 14 is extremely alkaline. The middle of the scale, 7.0, is neutral.

Maintaining a proper pH in the pool or spa is very important. Proper pH readings range from 7.2 to 7.8. Liquid (muriatic) or granular acid is used to lower pH levels. Alkaline substances such as baking soda or soda ash are used to raise pH levels.

Water reacts differently when it is too acidic or too alkaline. Low pH water (acidic) becomes corrosive and dissolves the metal it contacts. Acidic water is irritating to eyes and skin. Water that has high pH readings (alkaline) develops scale (calcium deposits) on equipment, plumbing, pool walls, and tiles. Additionally, alkaline water lessens the effectiveness of sanitizers in the pool.

Those with plaster-coated pools must add small amounts of acid to keep the pH down because a plaster pool contains an alkali that constantly dissolves into the pool. Acid is available in dry granular form or in liquid form (muriatic acid). If the pool surface is vinyl, fiberglass, or another impervious substance, there is no need to add acid because no alkaline substance is added to the water.

Caution: *Never mix alkalis and chlorine. The combination may result in a deadly chlorine gas.*

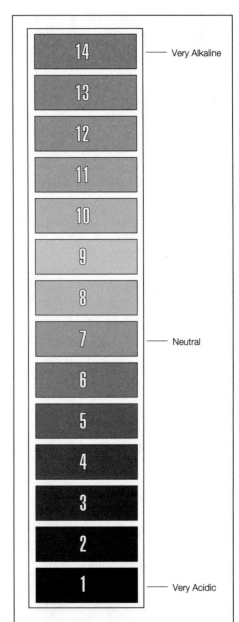

pH Levels. pH readings are used to estimate the relative alkalinity or acidity of water.

Test Procedure Guidelines

A test kit provides a description of exact procedures, but there are some basic procedures and precautions to follow regardless of the test conducted.

■ Check the reagents before they are used. Are they cloudy? Discolored? Is there precipitate on the bottom of the bottle? If there is, throw them away. Use only fresh test strips and reagents. Store them at moderate temperatures and never expose them for very long to direct sunlight. Buy fresh reagents each year.

■ Use pool water to rinse out the test kit vials before making a new test. Never use detergents to clean the vials. Chemical residue from soaps and detergents create false readings.

■ If chemicals have been added to the pool, wait several hours before taking additional test samples. Before chemicals can register completely they need time to circulate through the water. Make sure the circulation system has been running before the test is done. Observe and record test results immediately. The chemistry in water changes after sitting around for a while.

■ Handle reagents and samples carefully. Many contain toxic chemicals. Avoid direct contact and do not pour them into the pool or spa after the test is finished.

water in a clean tube and add test kit chemicals (called reagents) which create a color change in the sample. Then compare the sample with a color chart of known values. Typically the chart displays at least four different shades of each specified color—the stronger the color, the stronger the chemical presence.

Paper Strips. Color tests also are performed using paper strips that are impregnated with test chemicals.

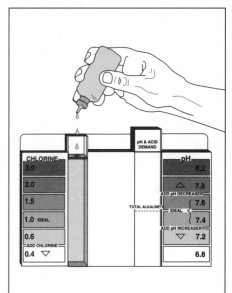

Reagents. Color testing with chemicals is the most common way to test pool water.

Additional Water Components

Other components of healthy water do not fluctuate as often as the sanitizer level, total alkalinity, and pH. Take a water sample to a pool supply store once or twice a year for a thorough analysis and recommended treatments for hardness (calcium hardness is a component of total alkalinity), total dissolved solids (a measurement of everything that has gone into the water but has not been filtered out), and cyanuric acid (a conditioner that is added to the pool once or twice a year to extend the life of the chlorine by shielding it from the sun's UV rays).

Testing the Water

Problems with the water balance in a pool and spa can be diagnosed by testing the water. Each component of water chemistry has its own test requirements. Test the water twice a week in the summer and once a week in the winter (if the pool is not closed or winterized). Test kits are available

at pool and spa supply stores and come with specific instructions for the testing and result analysis of water components.

Reagents. Color testing with chemicals is the most common way to test pool water. Collect a small amount of

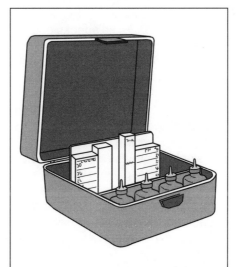

Testing the Water. Problems concerning the water balance can be diagnosed by testing the water.

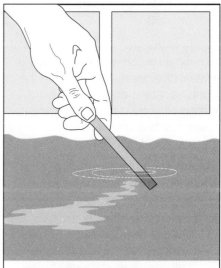

Paper Strips. Color tests also are performed using paper strips that are impregnated with test chemicals.

Correcting Water Chemistry Problems

Once you understand the components of water chemistry and how to test for specific problems, the challenge lies in correcting the discovered problems.

Types of Algae

There are over 20,000 known varieties of these one-celled plants. Algae thrives in sunlight and grows on steps and in corners or in other places where water circulation is not powerful. Algae is the yellow, brown, or green slime that resembles a thin layer of fur.

The conditions favorable for algae growth are: light (for photosynthesis), nutrients, high temperatures, and lack of sanitizers. Algae consumes the minerals in the pool for nutrients. Because the deeper water in the pool is cooler and not as bright, algae is found most often in the shallow areas of a pool. The following are three different forms of algae:

Green Algae (Chlorophyta). This is the most common form of algae. It grows as a broad, green slime on pool and spa surfaces. The slime can be removed by brushing, but only temporarily. The plant must be killed with chemicals.

Green algae first shows up on steps or in small patches in the corners. Take it as a warning signal that the pool is not properly maintained. Kill the algae at this stage. It grows extremely fast and can get out of control quickly.

Yellow Algae (Phaeophyta). This algae sometimes appears to be muddy brown. It may not grow as fast as green algae, but it is more difficult to kill. It grows in the same broad, mold-like pattern as green algae. Brushing removes the slimy outer layer and exposes the algae underneath to chlorine. The best killer, however, is superchlorination, called "shocking" the pool.

Brushing Algae. A combination of chemicals and scrubbing eliminates algae.

Black Algae (Cyanophyta). This algae is dark blue-green and is the worst form of pool algae. Black algae first appears as specks of dirt on the bottom of the pool. Unlike the other algae, it is unaffected by depth and sometimes shows up in the deepest part of the pool first. With time, the specks become bigger and spread all over the pool. While the initial rate of growth is slow, once it takes hold, it grows very fast. Black algae grows deeply into the plaster and concrete below. Use a stainless-steel brush to break open the hard surface and allow sanitizers and algicides to get in and do their job.

Brushing Algae

Some pool surfaces are easier to rid of algae than others. Smooth surfaces, such as fiberglass, come fairly clean simply by brushing. Algae, however, burrows in the cracks and crevices of rough surfaces so it is more difficult to clean a plaster surface. Usually a stain is left in the places that the brush cannot reach. Black algae forms a hard protective shell over itself, making it impenetrable to normal brushing.

Shocking the Pool

Algae sometimes grows in a pool even if water chemistry is maintained correctly. Superchlorination, or shocking, is the addition of heavy doses of sanitizer to eliminate bacteria and algae that normal maintenance does not destroy.

1 Preparing the Pool. When the pool is superchlorinated the water is circulated 24 hours a day until the residual returns to normal (between 1 and 3 parts per million as specified in the test kit). Turn on the pump and disengage the automatic time clock. The pool cannot be used during this process, so warn the family and post a sign to make sure no one uses it.

2 Shocking the Pool. Superchlorination requirements vary depending on the amount of use the pool gets and the form of chlorine being used. For liquid chlorine, 2 gallons per 5,000 gallons of pool water is a good rule of thumb. The label on the package of dry chlorine or other sanitizers explains how to shock the pool, but generally 5 to 7 times the normal amount of product is used.

3 Reopening the Pool. Depending on weather conditions and how much algae or other organic material is in the pool, it takes 24 to 48 hours for the high concentration of chlorine to dissipate to normal levels. Test the chlorine residual daily until the normal level is achieved. (Take water samples 12 to 18 inches below the surface.) Then resume normal pool use. Remember to replace the trippers on the automatic time clock and resume normal hours of circulation.

General Algae Elimination

Algae probably is the best reason for preventive maintenance (such as shocking and regular cleaning) and maintaining proper water chemistry. Getting rid of algae is much more difficult than doing everything necessary to avoid it. Keep the pool, baskets, and filter clean. Keep the chemicals balanced and brush the pool often even if algae and dirt are not apparent.

Unfortunately, algae has a way of growing even in the best maintained pools and spas. When algae does appear, there are two ways to deal with it. One is a general elimination program that works on most algae. The other is for more resistant algae (elimination combined with a special algicide). The following instructions explain how to eliminate normal algae:

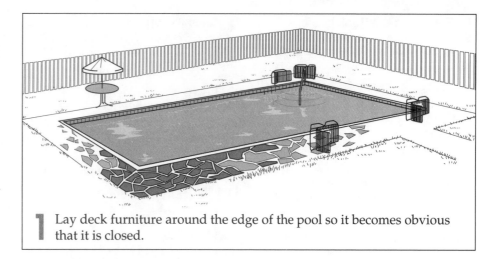

1 Lay deck furniture around the edge of the pool so it becomes obvious that it is closed.

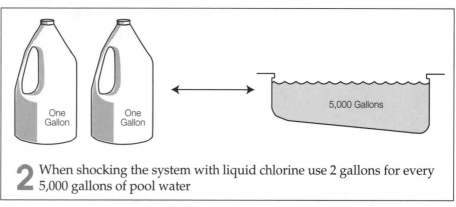

2 When shocking the system with liquid chlorine use 2 gallons for every 5,000 gallons of pool water

3 Test the chlorine residual daily until the normal level is achieved. Be sure to take water samples a minimum of 12 in. below the surface.

1 **Preparing the Pool.** Use a leaf net to clean the surface of the water. Dirt and leaves absorb sanitizers and work against an algae eradication program. Clean the skimmer and strainer pot, and break down and clean the filter (see pages 34-40). This step is essential because when the algae dies or is brushed from the sides of the pool, eventually it clogs the filter. The circulation system may have to be cleaned numerous times during the algae elimination process.

2 **Adding Trichlor.** Add 1 pound of trichlor for every 3000 gallons of water. Then use a wall brush clipped to a telepole to thoroughly brush the entire pool. This helps get rid of the algae and stirs up the trichlor. Check the pH and adjust if necessary. Never use trichlor on dark plaster or painted or vinyl pools—it discolors these surfaces. Instead, use 2 gallons of liquid chlorine for every 5,000 gallons of pool water.

Note: Do not leave chemical bottles on pool decks. Chemical stains are difficult, if not impossible, to remove. If a bottle has to be placed on a deck, dip it in the pool first to rinse off any chemicals. Then splash some water on the deck to neutralize residue.

3 **Cleaning up the Residue.** Run the circulation system for 72 hours and brush the pool at least once a day during this period. Do not use the pool during this procedure. Adjust the pH as needed. Add chlorine to maintain a chlorine residual of at least 6 parts per million. Keep a close eye on the filter pressure to make sure dead algae does not clog the filter. Vacuum the pool often

during treatment to remove dead algae and the inert ingredients of the trichlor. Both the dead algae and the inert ingredients look like white dust.

Allow the chlorine residual to return to 3 parts per million and resume a normal maintenance routine and normal use of the pool. Continue to brush often for the next week. Even if the algae is not apparent, it is still there waiting to bloom again.

1 Dirt and leaves absorb sanitizers and work against an algae eradication program.

Trichlor

2 Add 1 pound of trichlor for every 3000 gallons of water.

3 Vacuum the pool often during treatment to remove dead algae and the inert ingredients of the trichlor.

Elimination Guidelines for Persistent Algae

To remove more stubborn algae, such as the yellow or black species, use the following method.

1 **Brushing Algae.** Use a stainless-steel brush clipped to a telepole to vigorously brush the worst patches of algae. This breaks open the algae allowing chemicals to attack the plant more effectively. Brush the rest of the pool normally.

2 **Applying Trichlor to Algae.** Use a hollow telepole (or a length of 2-inch PVC pipe) to apply the granular trichlor directly to the algae. Hold the pole over a patch of algae and pour a cup of trichlor through the pole so that the chemical settles over the algae. (The pole also can be used to maneuver a chlorine tablet over the algae patch.) Use just enough for a light dusting. It may be necessary to turn off the pump so the water currents do not defeat the purpose of direct application.

When algae patches appear in a deeper location or on the side of a wall, use a stocking filled with trichlor or tablets and hang it in the pool over the patches. Do not worry about covering every inch of the algae. Just having a concentrated dose so close to it will do the trick.

Caution: *Do not use these techniques if you have a vinyl or dark-colored plaster pool. The concentration of chemicals weakens the vinyl and bleaches out the color.*

Algicides

Algicides are used to kill stubborn algae that is widespread or that keeps coming back. Stronger than trichlor, algicides fall into two basic categories: those for pools and those for spas. They are regulated by the U.S. Environmental Protection Agency and are considered pesticides. These products have been tested extensively so follow the instructions on the labels.

Generally, algicides come in liquid form and are poured into the skimmer while the pump is running. In this way they are distributed throughout the pool by way of normal circulation. To eliminate recurring problems, these products are used in addition to the chlorine-based techniques already described. Usually it is safe to swim in water that has been treated with algicide, but read the product label to be sure. Handling these products is harmless as long as they are not ingested. They have little odor or fumes. Do not drip or spill algicides around garden areas; they are, after all, designed to kill plants!

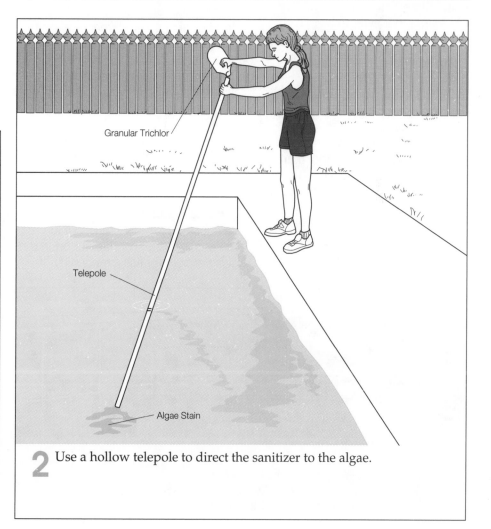

Stainless-Steel Brush

Algae Stain

1 Attach a stainless steel brush to a telepole and vigorously brush the most severe patches of algae.

Granular Trichlor

Telepole

Algae Stain

2 Use a hollow telepole to direct the sanitizer to the algae.

3 **Checking the Pool.** After one hour of direct contact between the algae growth and chlorine product, brush the algae again, working the trichlor into the algae and distributing the remaining product throughout the pool. Use a test kit to determine the effect this has on the overall chlorine residual. If it exceeds 3 parts per million, do not use the pool until it drops to that level or below. If not, continue regular maintenance and use of the pool. Unlike general algae elimination, the process of removing stubborn algae growth usually exists in a more limited area and therefore does not leave much residue behind.

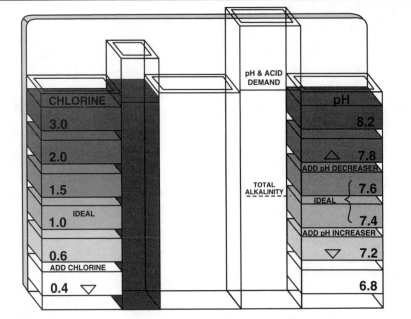

3 If the chlorine level exceeds 3 ppm do not use the pool.

Common Water Problems & Cures

Algae is the most common problem encountered in a pool or spa, but there are other symptoms that indicate water problems.

Colored Water. If the water turns color but there is no algae problem, there are metals in the water which must be removed. Green water indicates the presence of copper; brown or red indicates iron; brown or blackish water is a sign that manganese or silver is present. These metals come from metal fixtures which are slowly being dissolved by corrosive chemical conditions in the water.

The solution to these problems requires maintaining the pH or sanitizer level of the pool water and adding a chelating agent. A chelating agent is a liquid chemical that reacts with the metal in such a way that causes it to bind up in larger clumps so it can be filtered out of the water. A pool supply store can recommend the right chelating agent for each particular problem. Do not let this problem continue unabated as the water is unhealthy and you will eventually ruin your circulation system.

Cloudy Water. Cloudy water usually is caused by poor filtration which means that the filter has not been run long enough or it is simply dirty. If you have a diatomaceous earth (DE) filter, leaking DE can cloud the water (see pages 34-40). Check the filter grids for separated seams or holes. Check the alkalinity of the water. High readings result in clouding. For spas, it may mean a high total dissolved solids (tds) reading.

Scale. Scaling occurs when calcium carbonate precipitates out of the water by way of evaporation or heat. Check the calcium hardness level by purchasing a hardness test kit that works just like a chlorine test kit. If it is near or over 2000 parts per million, drain at least half the pool and replace the water. If it is below 2000 parts per million, the scale formation might be a result of a high pH or total alkalinity problem. Use a regular test kit to check pH and total alkalinity. Scale is a constant problem in spas that are used often. A combination of heat and high bather loads mean a heavy use of chemicals and a high level of evaporation. The water becomes hard (calcium laden) quickly. If this is a problem, change the spa water on a regular basis.

Eye or Skin Irritation. This problem can be traced to a low chlorine residual (also known as free chlorine)

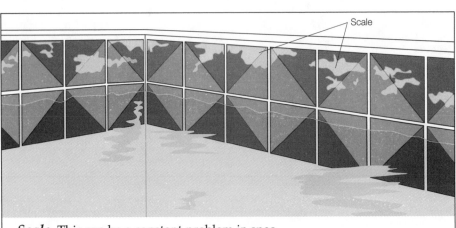

Scale. This can be a constant problem in spas.

in the water. Chlorine residual is the amount of chlorine available for sanitizing organic matter after the initial chlorine demand has been met. Other causes of irritation are low pH and too many chloramines. Chloramines are a combination of ammonia (which gets in the pool via perspiration) and chlorine. The result is a strong chlorine smell. (Chloramines cause the water to smell as if there is an abundance of chlorine in the water even though there is not.) Adjust the pH and shock the pool. The shocking process eliminates the chloramines.

Colored Hair, Nails, or Skin. Coloration of the body is caused by metals that are suspended in the water. Add a chelating agent to the water and check the pH to see if it has become too acidic. Bleaching of hair and bathing suits can be caused by heat and too much chlorine (a common problem in spas). Use a test kit to check chemistry levels. If the level of chlorine exceeds 3 parts per million reduce the amount of chlorine used.

Musty Odor. High bacteria or algae growth in a small spa causes a musty odor. Get rid of the algae by shocking the water to kill the bacteria, or just drain and refill the spa. A mildew-like smell might come from mildew found on a spa or deck cover or in wet crevices. Follow your nose to the source, and use household cleansers that contain chlorine bleach to get rid of the mildew.

Problems with Spa Water

Spas have the same problems as pools, but because of the high concentration of chemicals, bathers, and heat, a problem in the spa often intensifies and spreads more quickly.

Excessive Foam. Foam is caused by a combination of suntan oil, dirt, body oil, and the blower or jets. Of course, all kinds of soap also cause foaming. Drain and clean the spa and refill it with fresh water. Clean the filter as well, or the problem will not go away. Soap is difficult to remove

from a cartridge filter. Soak the cartridge overnight or replace it.

Skin Rash. Skin rashes and other irritations take place in spas that have high levels of bacteria. Rashes are made worse by heat and agitated water. Shock the water, or drain, clean, and refill the spa.

Spa Odor. A strong caustic odor is usually caused by a low pH rather than too much bromine. Adjust the pH, or drain some (or all) of the water and replace it.

Treating the Water

Follow the directions on the product label. In addition to the directions, the following are some general guidelines for administering pool chemicals:

Safety and freshness are the two most important guidelines. Pool chemicals are strong, so handle with care. (Pool chlorine is the same thing as laundry bleach, only five times stronger.) Chemicals, especially liquid chlorine, lose their potency over time, so buy smaller quantities frequently rather than an entire summer's supply all at once.

Liquids. There usually are four one-gallon bottles to a case of liquid chlorine. Chlorine comes in either heavy-duty reusable bottles and plastic cases that require a deposit or disposable bottles in cardboard cases. Because products differ in strength, always read the label.

Caution: *Do not get liquid chlorine on your skin or in your eyes. Use water to flush your eyes if splashed with chlorine. Rinse skin with water.*

Liquids. Stand on the diving board to reach the center of the pool.

Pour liquid chlorine as close as possible to the surface of the water or stand on the diving board so the center of the pool can be reached. Do not splash chlorine on yourself or the deck. Add it slowly near a return line with the pump running to help distribute it. Pour chlorine near the steps and in spots that have poor circulation. Never pour liquid chlorine directly into the skimmer.

Granulars. Alkaline materials, sanitizers (chlorine), and acids also come in granular form. Study the label to determine the amount to use and how to apply it. Granular products tend to settle to the bottom before completely dissolving. If the pool or spa is vinyl or dark plaster, it is best to brush it thoroughly until the product has dissolved. The undissolved product may cause discoloration. An alternative is to create a solution of the product by dissolving it in a bucket of water before adding it to the pool or spa. While granular products have a longer shelf life than liquids, they still are affected by age and direct sunlight.

Caution: *Never add a granular product directly to the skimmer. Avoid direct contact. These products are concentrated and can cause skin irritation and breathing problems. Handle them with care.*

Tabs and Floaters. Chlorine tablets slowly dissolve in floating devices. They are helpful for those who cannot check the pool often yet need a constant sanitizer. The tablets are expensive, however, and the rate of dissolution cannot be controlled. Like granular products, a tablet on the bottom of the pool discolors a vinyl or colored pool. Never leave a tablet in the skimmer. Tablets have a very low pH which means the equipment and related plumbing are subject to an acid bath.

Acids and Alkalis. When adding acid to a pool or spa, pour it close to the surface of the water to keep it from splashing onto the deck or onto your clothing and skin. If it does get on you, rinse the area immediately with fresh water. Seek medical

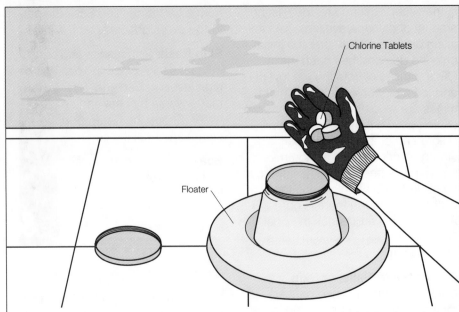

Tabs and Floaters. Tablets, as constant sanitizers, are useful for people who cannot check the pool as often as necessary.

Chlorine Tablets

Floater

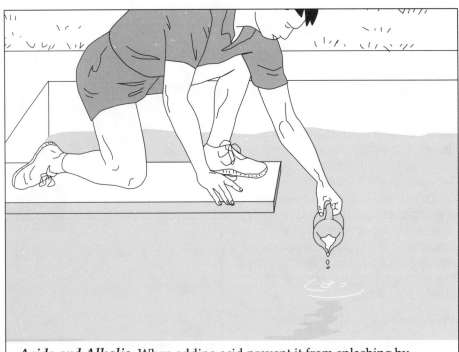

Acids and Alkalis. When adding acid prevent it from splashing by pouring it close to the surface of the water.

attention if acid gets in your eyes or if a burning rash persists after a water rinse.

When adding acid, dilute it as quickly as possible. Walk around the pool's deck as you add it. Adding it near a strong return outlet with the pump running gets it circulating fast. Never add acid near the skimmer, the main

drain, or a suction inlet. Full-strength acid eats away at pool equipment.

When adding soda ash or other alkaline materials, dissolve it in a bucket of water first, and then add it slowly to the pool. Adding too much too fast can turn the water a milky blue. Follow the directions on the package.

PUMPS & MOTORS

The three main elements of a pool or spa circulation system are the pump, filter, and heater. The pump and motor move water through a pool circulation system. Simple repair and basic maintenance keeps the system in good working order and ensures a healthy pool.

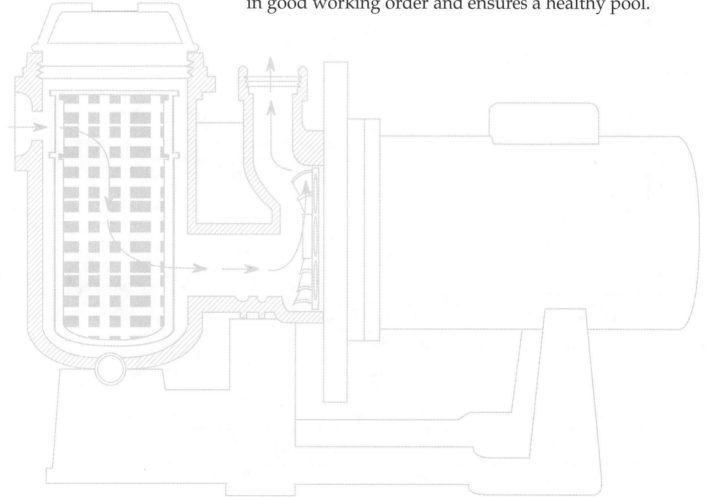

Pumps & Motors

Pool and spa pumps are centrifugal. As the impeller spins in the volute, it shoots out water thereby creating a vacuum that requires a continuous supply of water to equalize the force. In this way water is pulled from the pool where it takes a circular path through the pump, filter and heating units and then returns to the pool. To understand the pump you must first recognize its various components.

Strainer Pot and Basket. The plumbing from the pool's main drain and skimmer connects to the inlet port of the pump. The water flows into the strainer pot (also called the hair and lint trap) which holds a plastic mesh basket that is 4 to 6 inches in diameter and 5 to 9 inches deep. As water flows through the basket the mesh traps small debris. Baskets rest in the pot or twist-lock in place and most have handles to facilitate removal.

The strainer pot may be a separate component that is bolted to the volute or it may be molded to the volute to form one piece.

Many strainer pot covers are made of clear plastic so you can tell when the basket is full. The cover threads into the pot or it is held by two bolts that have a T-top or a handle for easy turning.

An O-ring lies between a strainer cover and the lip of the strainer pot to prevent suction leaks. A failed O-ring causes the pump to suck air rather than water from the pool.

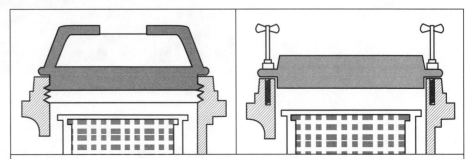

Strainer Pot and Basket. Some pumps have a cover that screws in place (left). Some strainer pot covers are held in place with two bolts that have a T-top or handle for easy turning (right).

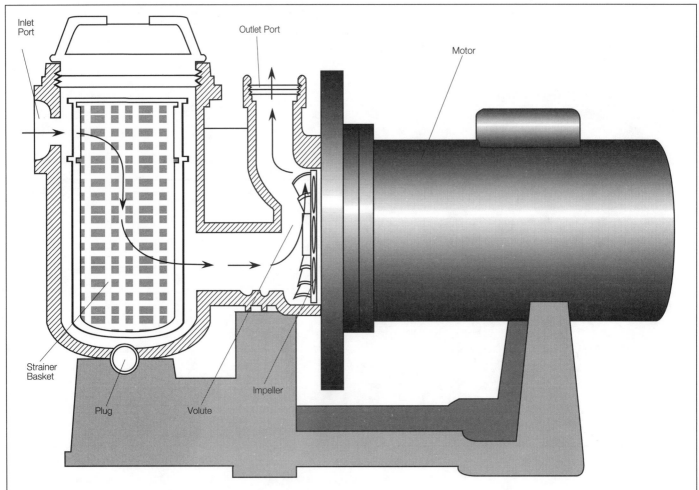

Pumps and Motors. Pool and spa pumps are centrifugal; as the impeller spins in the volute it shoots out water.

Notice the sacrificial plug that is screwed into the bottom of the pot. This plug allows the pot to be drained completely in preparation for winter. The material it is made from is weaker than the pot itself (usually plastic, soft lead, or brass is used). If the water in the pot freezes and expands, the plug pops out, relieving the pressure and preventing the pot from cracking.

Volute. The impeller spins inside the volute, forcing the water out of the pump and into the plumbing to the filter. The volute's female-threaded outlet port provides easy plumbing. The impeller sucks water from the strainer pot, creating a vacuum which is filled by water that rushes into the volute. The water is then directed out of the pump. The strainer pot is a vacuum (intake) chamber and the volute is a pressure (discharge) chamber.

Impeller. The impeller is the ribbed disk that spins inside the volute. The ribs are called vanes and the disk itself is called a shroud. As the water enters the center of the impeller the vanes force it to the outside edge of the disk. A drop in pressure occurs in the center as the water moves to the outside edge, creating a vacuum that becomes the actual suction of the pump. There are two basic impeller designs: semi-open and closed.

Seal Plate. To allow access to the impeller, the volute is divided into two sections: the rounded volute and the seal plate. The seal plate is joined to the volute with bolts or a clamp; a gasket or an O-ring is placed between them to make it watertight. The motor then bolts onto the seal plate. The motor shaft passes through a hole in the center of the seal plate and the impeller is threaded onto the end of the shaft. The shaft turns the impeller. Some shafts have extenders (held in place

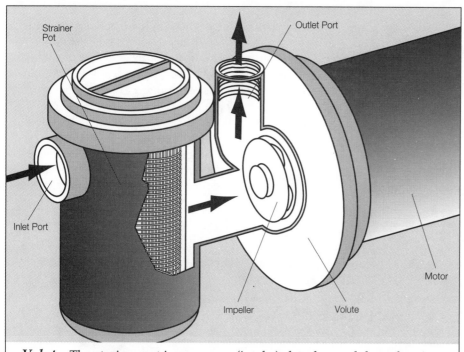

Volute. The strainer pot is a vacuum (intake) chamber and the volute is a pressure (discharge) chamber.

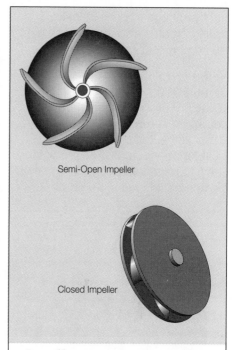

Impeller. This ribbed disk spins inside the volute.

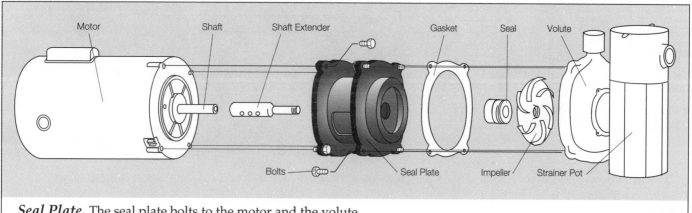

Seal Plate. The seal plate bolts to the motor and the volute.

with three Allen setscrews) that bridge from the motor to the impeller.

Seal. The pump has a shaft seal that prevents water from passing through the hole that the motor shaft fits through, into the motor. One half of the seal is made up of a rubber gasket (or O-ring) that is fitted around a ceramic ring and fits into a groove in the back of the impeller. The ceramic ring can withstand high temperatures caused by friction. The other half of the seal is made of a metal bushing and a spring that fits into a groove in the seal plate. Heat-resistant graphite covers the end of the spring that faces the ceramic ring. The seal fits tightly enough to prevent leaks. The spring creates a watertight seal by putting pressure on both halves.

Motors. The most common ratings for pool and spa motors range from 0.5 to 2.0 horsepower. Motors are designed to run on either 110 or 220 volts. A variety of motors are built for pool pumps. The motor face (be it C-frame or square flange) must be compatible to the pump design.

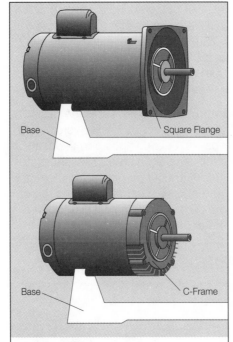

Motors. The motor face, be it C-frame or square flange, must be compatible to the pump design.

Cleaning Strainer Pots

This is the easiest, and one of the most important, of pump maintenance procedures. Clean the basket frequently. It does not take much to clog up the mesh and slow down water flow.

1 Taping the Breakers. Turn off the circuit breaker that powers the pump and place tape over it so no one accidentally turns it on while you are working.

2 Cleaning the Basket. Remove the clamps or bolts from the strainer pot cover. Remove the basket from the strainer pot and clean it thoroughly. If the basket or pot is cracked or broken, replace it. Large pieces of debris can pass through a hole and, in turn, jam the impeller and clog the plumbing.

3 Closing the Pot. Turn the power back on. Replace the basket and fill the strainer pot with water so the pump can prime (as described on page 27). Before replacing the lid check the O-ring for cracks or tears. Replace the cover and tighten the bolts or clamps. Start the pump to check that water is circulating normally. If the water is not moving in the pool within two

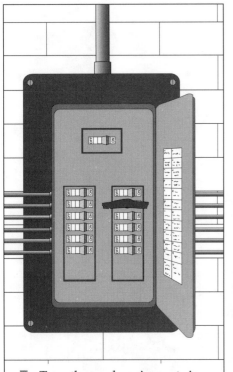

1 Turn the pool equipment circuit breaker to the "off" position. Put tape over it to prevent it being switched on accidentally.

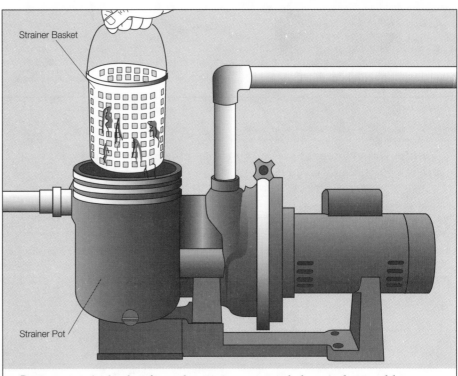

2 Remove the basket from the strainer pot and clean it thoroughly.

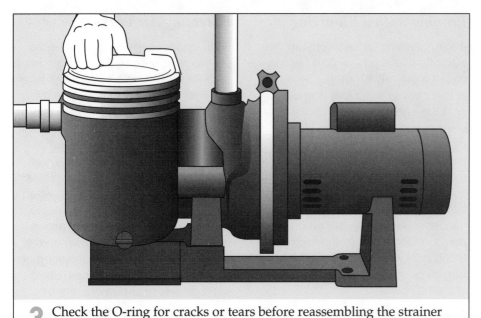

3 Check the O-ring for cracks or tears before reassembling the strainer pot basket and lid.

1 Checking for Obstructions.

The path of the water must be free of obstructions. With the pump turned off, open the strainer pot lid and remove the basket and dispose of the leaves and debris. Check that all the valves are open and make sure there are no blockages in the plumbing or equipment. The buoyant, hinged plate at the opening of the skimmer is called the weir. The weir allows only a thin layer of surface water into the skimmer. Check that the weir is free of debris. Use the telepole and net to scoop debris off the main drain.

2 Filling the Pot.

Fill the strainer pot with water until it overflows. Put the lid on tightly so air cannot enter. If the pump is above the water level of the pool, the fill water may drain into the pool as you pour it in. If it seems to be flowing out as fast as it is filled, fill it as high as possible and replace the lid.

3 Starting the Motor.

Start the motor and open the air relief valve found at the top of the filter. The pump is primed when normal circulation begins and water dis-

to three minutes, the pump may have to be primed.

Priming the Pump

Priming is starting the suction that gets water moving through the pump thus creating circulation in the pool. Modern pool pumps are self-priming, but sometimes they need a little help if the water has drained out of the pump and/or plumbing during servicing.

Before restarting a pump that has been serviced, or one that has been off for a while, check the water level in the pool. Water is sometimes lost during maintenance and there might not be enough in the pool to fill the skimmer. Some pools require the water to be at the very top of the skimmer before the pump primes.

1 The path of the water must be free of obstructions. Lean over the deck edge to clear the skimmer weir.

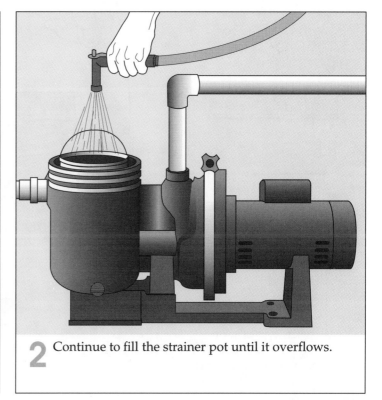

2 Continue to fill the strainer pot until it overflows.

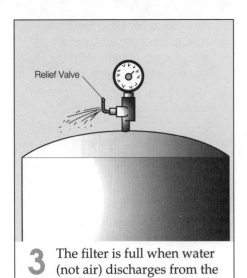

3 The filter is full when water (not air) discharges from the relief valve.

places the air in the filter. Wait about two minutes for the pump to become primed, but do not overheat it by running a dry pump. If normal circulation does not start, fill water in the pot two or three times to get it going. Airlocks sometimes occur on hot days when the air expands in the pipe. Repeat the procedure to remove the air.

Priming with a Blow Bag

If normal priming does not start the water flow, use a blow bag (also called a drain-flush bag). One end of this canvas or rubber bag screws onto the end of a garden hose. The other end of the blow bag fits into the skimmer hole that feeds the pump. Turn on the hose. The bag expands and seals the skimmer hole, feeding water from the hose into the pump. Run the water for a minute or two and then turn on the pump. When water and air returns to the pool, quickly pull out the blow bag so pool water takes the place of the hose water.

Note: The blow bag does not work if the skimmer has just one hole in the bottom that connects to the pump and the main drain. The forced water from the blow bag simply escapes down the main drain and bypasses the pump altogether. A blow bag must be placed in a skimmer hole that is plumbed directly to the pump.

Detecting Air Leaks

If the system experiences repeated problems in priming itself, it may have an air leak. After the system has been circulating water normally, shut it off and listen to the equipment. Hissing or gurgling sounds suggest air leaks. Check for water around the pump, filter, and heater. A small water leak that occurs when the water circulation is operating allows air to get in when the system is turned off. In turn, the air that leaks into the system allows water to drain into the pool when the equipment is turned off. Repairing an air leak usually is as easy as replacing a gasket or O-ring or tightening a strainer pot lid. (See page 26.)

Maintenance & Repairs

The best tools for taking care of a motor and pump are your ears and eyes. Listen to the motor. Is it laboring? Are there leaks in or around the pump? It is important to keep the motor dry and cool and the pump free from leaks.

Replacing Pump Gaskets

If a gasket leaks, disassemble the strainer pot from the volute and replace it. Purchase a new strainer pot gasket at a pool supply store. (Write down the manufacturer and model number of the pump before you go.)

1 Disconnecting the Pump Plumbing. Some plumbing has threaded unions that make disassembling a pump as simple as unscrewing a fitting. Most systems, however, are plumbed and require a simple cut. If so, use a hacksaw to cut the PVC on the discharge side of the pump only. Leave a few inches of pipe on each side of the cut for reassembly.

2 Disassembling the Pump. Use a 1/2- to 9/16-inch box wrench (depending on the model of pump) to unbolt the strainer pot from the

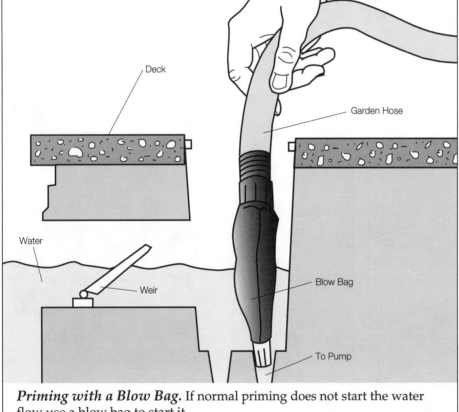

Priming with a Blow Bag. If normal priming does not start the water flow use a blow bag to start it.

volute. Separate the two pump components to expose the strainer pot gasket.

3 Replacing the Gasket. Use a flat-blade screwdriver to scrape away the old gasket on the volute. Clean away all traces of the old gasket (gaps cause leaks) and replace the gasket with a new one. Older or corroded pumps may require two rubber gaskets to fill the gaps. Paper-type gaskets expand slightly when soaked in warm water before installation. Coat the pump halves with silicone in the places they touch the gasket. Use only nonhardening silicone lubricants available at pool supply stores or scuba diving shops. Vaseline and other petroleum based lubricants eat plastic and paper.

4 Reassembling the Pump. Tighten the bolts evenly (first one side, then the opposite, a little each time) so the compression of the gasket is even. Do not overtighten the bolts found on plastic pumps.

5 Connecting the Discharge Pipe. Use a slip coupling and PVC solvent cement to replumb the discharge pipe. Check for leaks at the pipe union and reattach if necessary.

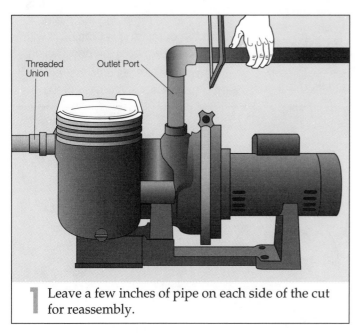

1 Leave a few inches of pipe on each side of the cut for reassembly.

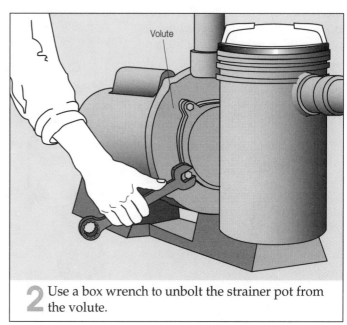

2 Use a box wrench to unbolt the strainer pot from the volute.

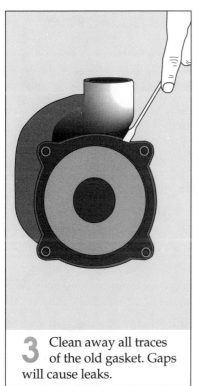

3 Clean away all traces of the old gasket. Gaps will cause leaks.

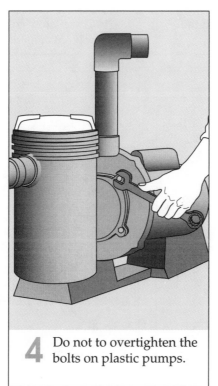

4 Do not to overtighten the bolts on plastic pumps.

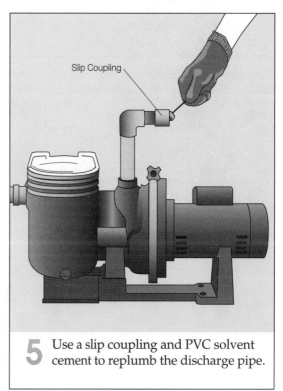

5 Use a slip coupling and PVC solvent cement to replumb the discharge pipe.

Creating PVC Pipe Unions

PVC pipe sections are joined with a fitting and solvent cement. When properly done the union is completely watertight. The process of connection is very simple. Be sure the pipes are cut clean at 90 degrees and lightly sanded before joining them.

1 Priming the Pipe. The purpose of PVC primer is to clean the parts that are going to be joined by the fitting. Spread a liberal amount of primer inside the fittings as well as around the outside ends of the pipes.

Caution: *Work in a ventilated area, and wear eye protection and gloves.*

2 Applying the Cement. While the primer is still wet, apply a heavy coat of PVC solvent cement to the outside end of each pipe and to the insides of the fitting. Cover the surfaces completely.

3 Joining the Pipes. Slide the two pipes into the fitting to create a solid length of pipe. Twist the fitting back and forth several times, then hold the parts tightly together for about 20 seconds. This motion evenly spreads the solvent, covering the entire joint and ensuring a tight fit.

4 Creating a Seal. Work quickly to get the pieces locked together before the solvent hardens. The solvent cement must form a continuous bead around the joints or leaks will develop.

Replacing a Motor

Hundreds of dollars can be saved by replacing a faulty motor rather than purchasing a new pump system. Replacing the motor in a pump with a shaft extender is a common repair and is easier than it may seem. It is as simple as removing the motor from the pump and replacing it with a compatible model. Depending on the model, there are two ways to do it.

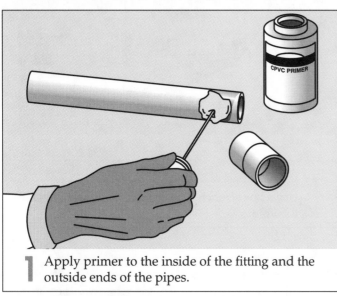

1 Apply primer to the inside of the fitting and the outside ends of the pipes.

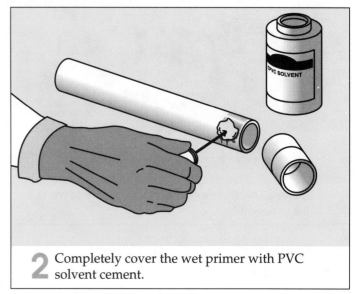

2 Completely cover the wet primer with PVC solvent cement.

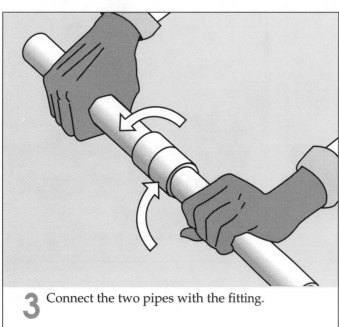

3 Connect the two pipes with the fitting.

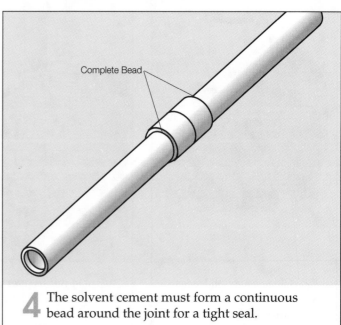

Complete Bead

4 The solvent cement must form a continuous bead around the joint for a tight seal.

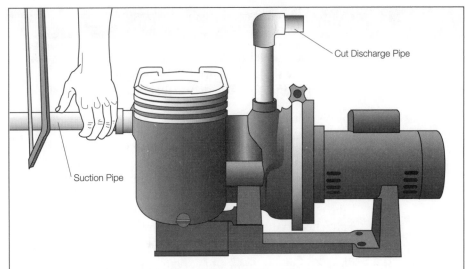

Removing the Motor (no shaft extender). Use a hacksaw to cut the plumbing at the discharge outlet and then at the suction inlet. Remove the pump, and take the entire unit to a technician.

Caution: *Before beginning work, turn off the electrical circuit breaker. Tape the breaker in the "off" position.*

Removing the Motor (no shaft extender)

If the pump does not have a shaft extender, the job requires disassembling the pump, impeller, seal, and seal plate. This is a complicated job that requires a good deal of precision and practice. Remove the entire pump or motor assembly and take it to the pool supply store where they can replace the motor.

Use a hacksaw to cut the plumbing at the discharge and suction pipes. Leave a few inches of pipe on each side of the cut to facilitate the slip couplings that are to go over each side. Disconnect the electrical connection. (Follow Step 2 of next procedure.) Take the unit to a technician. To install the new pump and motor, reverse the procedure.

Removing the Motor (with shaft extender)

1 **Removing the Old Motor.** Tape the breaker in the off position. Unbolt then remove the motor from the shaft extender by loosening the Allen-head screws and pulling the motor shaft out of the extender. If it is stuck use a large flat-blade screwdriver to pry it off.

2 **Disconnecting the Electrical Connection.** The electrical connection must be removed before the old motor can be disengaged. With the breaker taped in the "off" position, the access cover can be safely removed from the rear of the motor. The access cover is located near the hole where the electrical conduit enters. Remove the three wires and unscrew the conduit connector from the motor housing. Pull away the wiring and the conduit. If there is an additional ground wire (bonding wire), remove it by loosening the screw or clamp that holds it in place. Use electrical tape to tape off the ends of the exposed (disconnected) wires.

Do not turn on the breaker while the pump and motor are disconnected. Write a note of warning and tape it to the breaker box.

3 **Preparing the New Motor.** Take the old motor to a pool supply store to ensure that the new motor is compatible. Before reassembling, clean the new motor shaft with a fine emery cloth. Then apply a thin coat of silicone lube.

4 **Installing the New Motor.** Reconnect the electrical wires and conduit, then slide the shaft of the new motor into the shaft extender. Line up the setscrews of the shaft extender so they slide into the channel in the motor shaft. Bolt the motor to the bracket. Adjust the impeller by

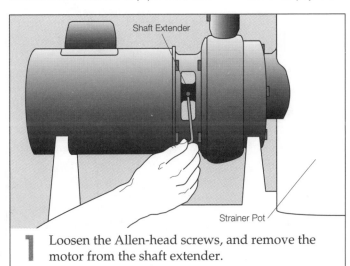

1 Loosen the Allen-head screws, and remove the motor from the shaft extender.

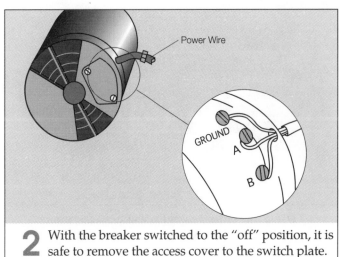

2 With the breaker switched to the "off" position, it is safe to remove the access cover to the switch plate.

A number of motor problems can be diagnosed by sight and sound. Many of the common problems with motors are remedied easily by replacing one part rather than replacing an entire motor.

■ **Flooding.** There are as many ways to soak a motor as there are pools. If it happens to yours, cut the supply of electricity to the motor immediately by turning off the circuit breaker. Wait 24 hours for the motor to air-dry before starting it again. Wet windings may cause a short.

◙ **Motor Will Not Start.** Check the breakers, and look for loose connections to the motor. Check the supply wires that are connected to the motor switch plate. Are they dirty? Dirt creates resistance, which causes heat. Heat melts wires and breaks the connection. If a supply wire is too small for the load it carries, it will overheat and melt, so replace them if necessary. Clean the dirty switch plate terminals, and reconnect the wiring.

■ **Loud Noises or Vibrations.** Remove the impeller, and briefly run the motor. If the motor still vibrates or makes a loud sound, the bearings are bad. The motor can be rebuilt with new bearings, but the cost is probably the same as that for buying a new motor. Unless the motor is still under warranty or relatively new, replace it. A bent shaft also causes this problem, but as in the case with the bad bearings, the cost of replacing the motor is little more than replacing the shaft alone.

■ **Motor Hums but Will Not Run.** The impeller may be jammed with debris. Turn off the breaker, and spin the shaft by hand. Remove debris that blocks the impeller.

If the impeller is not obstructed, check the capacitor. Symptoms of a bad capacitor include a liquid discharge or white residue. To replace the capacitor, remove the cover that holds it on top of the motor. This cover is held in place with two screws. On some motors it is mounted inside the end-cover, which also is held on the motor with two or three screws. The two wires are attached to the capacitor with simple push-on and pull-off bayonet clips. Install a new capacitor.

The motor may hum and yet fail to run because of insufficient line voltage. For example, the 120 volts may be coming in at only 100 volts owing to a bad breaker or a supply problem that originates at the electric company. Use a multimeter to check the actual voltage. Consult the utility company if there is a problem.

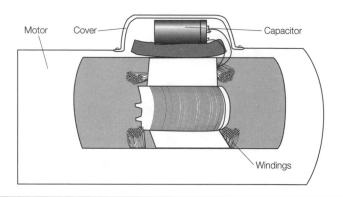

Motor   Cover   Capacitor   Windings

pressing it against the bracket. Use a screwdriver to apply pressure on the shaft extender. The spring that is located in the seal provides pressure against the screwdriver. Allow just enough space between the back of the impeller and the face of the bracket to permit the impeller to spin freely. Holding the impeller in this position, use an Allen wrench to tighten the screws. When they are tight, release the screwdriver, and check that the impeller and motor shaft spins freely.

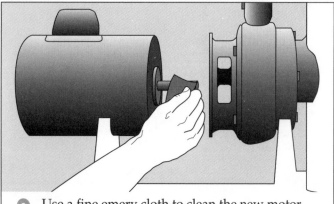

3 Use a fine emery cloth to clean the new motor shaft. Coat shaft with silicone lube.

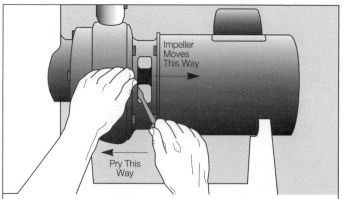

Impeller Moves This Way

Pry This Way

4 Adjust the impeller by pressing it against the bracket. Use a screwdriver to apply pressure on the shaft extender.

FILTER SYSTEMS

As water pumps through the circulation system of a pool or spa, impurities are strained by a filter. The filter itself has no moving parts and is made of simple components. As simple as it may be, a well-maintained filter is the secret to a healthy, sparkling pool.

Types of Filters

There are three basic types of filters: diatomaceous earth (DE), sand, and cartridge. Proper care and cleaning keep the filter efficient, and in turn, the pool or spa water clean.

Diatomaceous Earth (DE) Filters

Water passes through a tank in this filter which contains a series of fabric-covered grids (also called "filter elements"). The fabric is coated with a filtration substance media called DE, or diatomaceous earth.

DE is the fine, white powder remains of billions of prehistoric, microscopic organisms and is found in large deposits in the ground. Under a microscope these tiny particles look like sponges. Like a sponge, DE allows water to filter through while leaving impurities behind. These "sponges" are so small that they are able to filter out microscopic particles.

The right-sized filter is determined by the square footage of surface area of the filter media (either DE, sand, or cartridge). For DE filters, size equals the total square footage of the grids. The typical filter has eight grids that total 24 to 72 square feet. The grids are placed into tanks that are 2 to 5 feet high and about 2 feet in diameter. Filters also are classified according to how many gallons of water flow through them per minute.

A filter must be properly sized to a pool or spa's circulation system.

Without the filter grids, DE would turn into a caked mass when wet, making it impossible for water to flow through. There are two basic types of DE filters: the vertical grid and the spin type.

Vertical Grid Filters. The grids in this type of filter are assembled vertically on a manifold. A holding wheel secures the grids to the manifold and a retaining rod screws into the base of the tank to secure the assembly. Water enters the tank at the bottom and flows up and around the outside of the grids. It then flows down the stem of each grid, into the hollow manifold, and out of the filter.

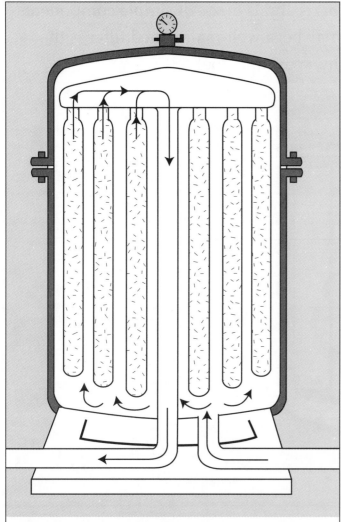

Diatomaceous Earth (DE) Filters. In this filter, the water passes through a series of fabric-covered grids that are coated with DE.

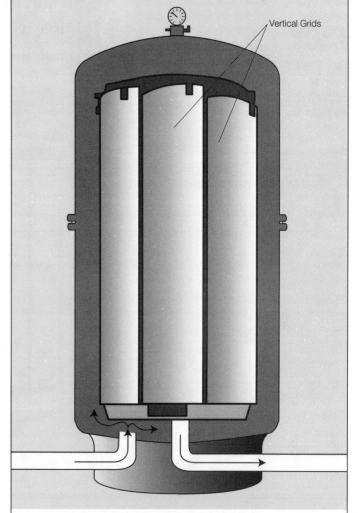

Vertical Grids

Vertical Grid Filters. The grids found in this filter are assembled vertically on a manifold.

Spin Filters. The spin filter is obsolete but still can be found on older pool systems. The grids are wheel shaped and lined up horizontally like a box of donuts. They operate in a similar manner to the vertical grid filter, but to clean them, a crank is turned to spin the grids. Although this is supposed to clean the grids, it is not very effective.

Sand Filters

Sand filter tanks are 2 to 4 feet in diameter and look like large balls. Older models generally are housed in metal tanks. The sand in a sand filter strains out impurities as the water pushes its way through.

The water enters the top or side of the filter through a multiport or piston backwash valve and sprays over the sand. The sharp edges of the grains catch the impurities. The water is pushed through the laterals and bottom manifold where it is then directed out of the filter. The individual drains of the drain manifold are called laterals. A drain pipe is located in the bottom of the tank for emptying out the water when necessary.

Cartridge Filters

The operation of a cartridge filter is similar to that of a DE filter except there is no DE involved. Water flows into the tank which houses one or more cylindrical cartridges of fine, pleated mesh material (usually polyester). The tight mesh of the fabric strains out impurities. Unlike the backwashing method used by DE and sand filters, when it is time to clean the cartridges they simply are removed and washed.

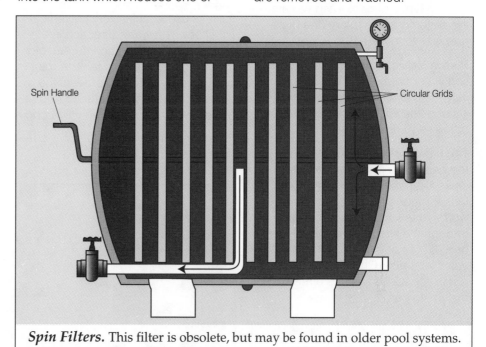

Spin Filters. This filter is obsolete, but may be found in older pool systems.

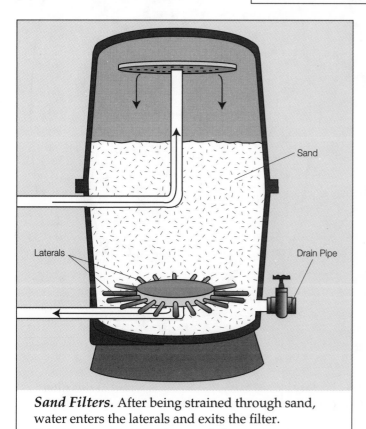

Sand Filters. After being strained through sand, water enters the laterals and exits the filter.

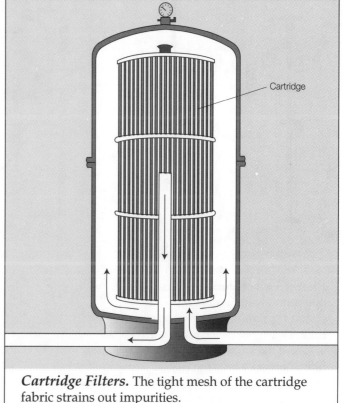

Cartridge Filters. The tight mesh of the cartridge fabric strains out impurities.

Backwashing

This process is used to clean DE and sand filters. The water is sent backwards through the filter, flushing the debris into a waste line or a sewer line. A backwash valve on the filter reverses the flow of the water. There are two types of backwash valves: the piston and the rotary (the multiport is a variation of the rotary valve).

Piston Valve. During normal operation water enters this piston-type valve and is directed to the filter. The water is then filtered through the DE or the sand and returns to the pool.

The handle of the piston is raised into the backwash position. The piston disks force the water into the filter tank through the outlet port. In other words, the water flows backward through the filter and flushes debris and dirt out of the tank and out of the valve inlet port. Once inside the valve again, the waste water is directed to the waste port.

Never change the piston position when operating the pump. This puts too much pressure on the pump, motor, and the valve O-rings, and may result in leaks. The piston-type backwash valve usually is located on the side of the filter tank.

Rotary Valve. The rotary backwash valve is used exclusively on vertical DE filters. The water direction is changed by rotating an internal rotor located below the filter tank. A rotor gasket seal or O-rings prevent the water from leaking. A retainer ring (inside the filter) holds the valve body to the underside of the tank with bolts that pass through the bottom of the tank.

To backwash, rotate the rotor 90 degrees. Water enters through the middle and up the inside of the grids. The DE and dirt is washed off the grids as the water flows from inside the grids to the outside. The water is then flushed back through the rotor and directed to the opening marked "backwash." Do not rotate the rotor while the pump is running—leaks may occur.

Multiport Valve. The multiport backwash valve is used on sand filters and looks like a rotary valve when taken apart. Sometimes mounted on the side but usually mounted on top of the filter tank, this valve offers more than one choice for water flow

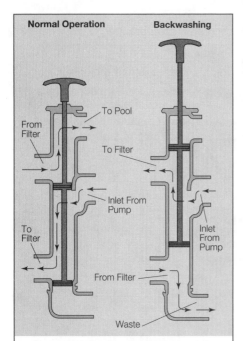

Piston Valve. During normal operation, water enters this piston-type valve and goes to the filter. During backwashing, water is forced backwards through the filter. Never change the piston position when the pump is operating—leaks will occur.

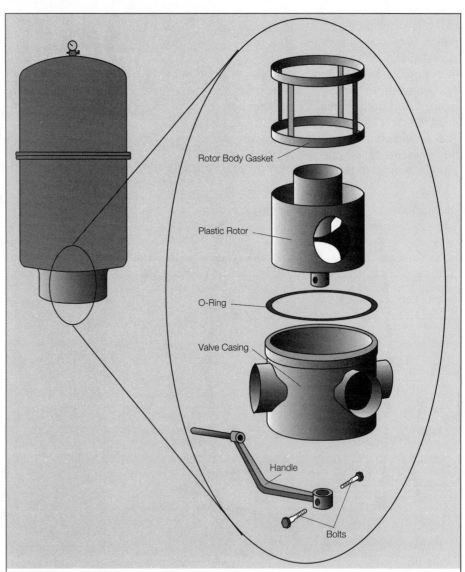

Rotary Valve. The rotary backwash valve is used exclusively on vertical DE filters.

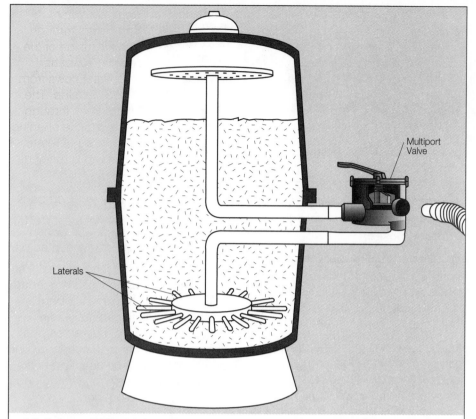

Multiport Valve. The multiport backwash valve is used mostly on sand filters and offers more than one choice for water flow direction.

60 pounds per square inch (psi). The normal operating pressure usually is approximately 15 psi. Use a marker to indicate normal operating pressure on your gauge. As a filter becomes dirty and clogs it takes more pressure for the water to flow and the gauge rises. Manufacturers recommend backwashing the filter when the pressure rises higher than 10 pounds above the normal, clean operating pressure.

1 Preparing the Filter. Turn off the pump and raise the piston backwash valve (or rotate the multiport valve) to the "backwash" position. Make sure the waste drain is open or attach the backwash hose.

2 Backwashing. Turn on the pump and watch the water through the sight glass. A sight glass is a clear section of pipe used to view the effectiveness of backwash-

direction. After the pump backwashes, clean water rinses out the pipes before returning to normal circulation. This prevents debris from returning to the pool after a backwash has been done.

Regardless of the valve used, if the backwash discharge port is not

plumbed directly to a drain or sewer line, a hose has to be attached to direct the dirty water onto the lawn or into the street. The normal hose usually is 1½ to 2 inches in diameter and made out of inexpensive, collapsible plastic. Backwash hoses are available in various lengths up to 200 feet. The pool vacuum hose can be turned into a backwash hose by using a hose clamp to attach it to the waste port of the backwash valve.

Dirty filter water is an excellent fertilizer. It is rich in nutrients and DE, and if the chlorine level is below 3 parts per million (see page 13) it is okay to run the backwash hose on the lawn or garden. Use a chlorine test kit to determine if the waste water is suitable—levels above 3 parts per million can burn grass.

Backwashing the Filter

A pressure gauge is mounted to the top of the filter or sometimes on the multiport valve. The gauge reads water pressure, expressed from 0 to

Backwashing the Filter. When the filter pressure rises 10 lbs. above the normal, clean operating pressure, it is time to backwash.

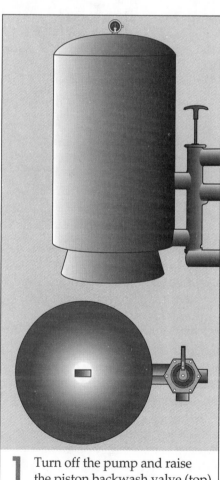

1 Turn off the pump and raise the piston backwash valve (top), or rotate the multiport valve to the "backwash" position (bottom).

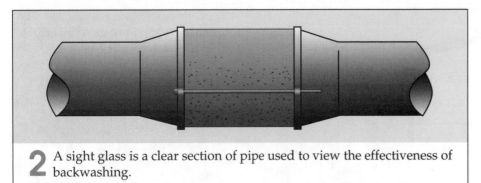

2 A sight glass is a clear section of pipe used to view the effectiveness of backwashing.

3 Push down the piston valve (top) or reset the multiport valve (bottom) and restart the pump for normal operation.

ing and can be installed anyplace you want to be able to check the quality of the water. The water first appears clean becoming gradually dirtier until it becomes filthy, and then slowly it becomes clear again. When it is reasonably clear turn off the pump. If the filter has a multiport valve turn it to the "rinse" position. Then turn on the pump and run water through this rinse cycle for 30 sec-

onds to flush dirt from the plumbing. Turn off the pump and rotate it back to the "filter" position.

3 **Restarting Normal Circulation.** Push down the piston valve (or rotate the multiport valve) to the normal filtration position and restart the pump for normal operation.

After backwashing use the pressure gauge to detect problems in the system. If the pressure is low something may be obstructing the water as it enters the filter. If the pressure is high the filter media may need to be changed or something may be hindering the water as it exits the filter. If the pressure fluctuates while the pump is running, the water level may be low, or there may be an obstruction in the skimmer.

Some filters are fitted with a separation tank. When the filter is backwashed the waste water is sent into this chamber and the dirt and used DE are strained from the water. The system may be plumbed to a sewer or it may require a backwash hose to divert the waste water from the separation tank to an appropriate drain. After backwashing, crack open the tank and empty the contents of the bag (the same way the bag on a household vacuum cleaner is emptied). Lift out the fabric grids, check for holes in the fabric, and hose them off.

Filter Repair & Maintenance

Filters are relatively easy to repair since they do not have moving parts. Regardless of the type of repair being

made to the filter, always relieve the internal pressure by opening the air relief valve. (This is called "bleeding" the air.) Always bleed the air from the filter before disassembling a component, because even when turned off, the pressure may be high enough to be dangerous.

Adding DE

After the backwashing process is done, the DE that washed out with the dirt must be replaced. Never run a DE filter without DE—not even for a short time. Without DE, the grids cannot filter out the dirt and they become clogged. Check the label on the filter to figure out how much DE is needed, or refer to the table on a DE bag. A one-pound coffee can makes an excellent DE scoop, but remember, DE is much lighter than coffee—a one-pound coffee can holds only a half a pound of DE. Twelve measuring cups of DE equals one pound.

With the pump on, add the DE through the skimmer. Do not dump it in all at once, however, as this will clog plumbing elbows and inlets on the filter tank. Sprinkle in one can at a time and use your hand to mix it with the skimmer water. DE appears

Adding DE. A one-pound coffee can holds 1/2 pound of DE (top). Add DE through the skimmer opening (bottom).

to dissolve, but it is suspended in the water. This keeps it from clumping.

Add the first can of DE and then wait a minute. Observe the pool circulation. If a cloud of DE is flowing into the pool it means there is a leak in the grids or other internal components of the filter. Do not add more DE, but shut off the pump and call a professional pool technician. Sometimes the backwashing loosens the grids or causes other internal leaks. If you do not know how to disassemble the filter it is best to call a technician.

Note: To solve the problem of adding too much DE too fast, use a slurry. Mix the DE in a bucket of water to achieve the suspension of the DE before pouring the solution into the skimmer.

Bridging. Beware of a condition known as bridging. This occurs when the filter is so dirty that the dirt buildup and the DE combine to bridge the normal spaces between the grids, leaving very little room for water. Bridging occurs after many years of use, and when DE is added without removing and completely cleaning the filter grids. If the filter pressure is too high and backwashing does not seem to help it may be a case of bridging. Call a service person to disassemble the filter and clean the internal components.

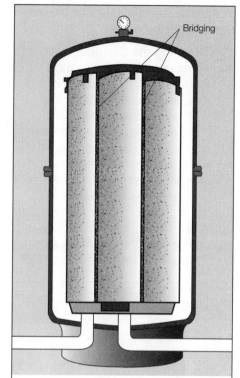

Bridging. When the dirt and DE combine to cover the normal spaces between the grids, a condition called bridging has occurred.

Correcting Channeling

Channeling occurs in sand filters when sand has calcified or clumped up due to chemical exposure, pressure, and dissolved pool plaster. Less water is filtered through these clumps than passes around them.
To prevent channeling, clean the filter after every third backwash.

1 Disassembling the Multiport Valve. Turn off the pump and bleed out the air pressure. Unscrew the threaded union collars and disconnect the multiport valve plumbing. (Unlike pump plumbing which usually is fixed, sand filters always are plumbed with unions as the unions are a part of the multiport valve.) Remove the valve from the tank. Some valves are bolted on, others are threaded into the body of the tank. If the filter has a large basket just inside the tank, remove it and clean it. If the filter has a piston-type backwash valve it will be mounted on the side and will not be in the way of removing the tank lid in order to gain access to the sand.

2 Breaking Apart the Sand. Push a garden hose inside the tank and flush the sand. Use a broom handle to break up clumps, but do not hit the fragile laterals on the bottom of the tank. Let the water fill and then overflow the tank, taking dirt and debris with it.

When the sand is completely free of clumps and suspended in the water turn off the garden hose. Replace the basket (if any), multiport valve, and

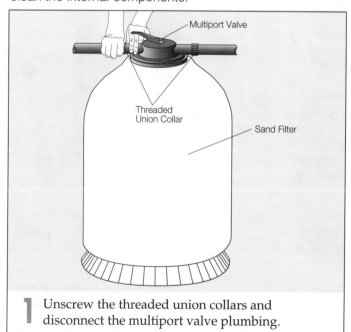

1 Unscrew the threaded union collars and disconnect the multiport valve plumbing.

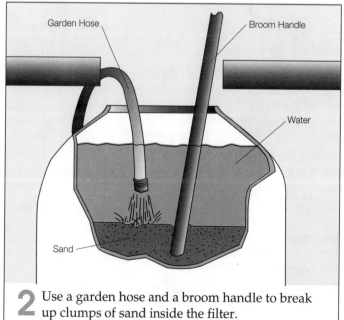

2 Use a garden hose and a broom handle to break up clumps of sand inside the filter.

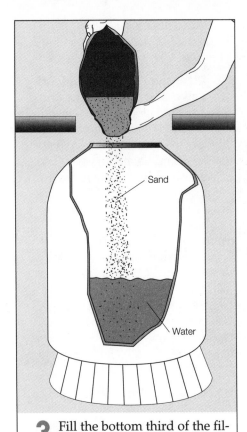

3 Fill the bottom third of the filter with water to provide a cushion for the laterals from the weight of the new sand.

plumbing. Backwash again briefly to clean out dislodged dirt.

3 **Adding Sand.** Look in the filter to check if some of the sand was lost during the backwashing. If so, add fresh sand. Every few years the sand needs to be replaced; it becomes less coarse with time and does not filter as well.

To add sand, fill the bottom third of the filter with water to provide a cushion for the laterals from the weight of the new sand. Most sand filters are filled about two-thirds with sand. Always backwash after adding new sand to remove dust and impurities.

Cleaning Cartridge Filters

Cartridge filters do not require backwashing. To clean a cartridge filter the entire filter cartridge must be removed.

1 **Disassembling the Filter.** Turn off the pump and bleed out the air. Remove the retaining band and lift the filter tank or lid from the base. Remove the cartridge.

2 **Cleaning the Cartridge.** Hose off light debris from the cartridge and examine inside the pleats where dirt sometimes accumulates. Never use pure acid, such as the muriatic acid used in pool chemistry, to clean a cartridge. Acid can cause organic material to harden in the fabric, making it almost waterproof. Instead, use a clean pail or garbage can to soak the cartridge for one hour in water that contains a diluted mixture of muriatic acid (1 cup acid per 5 gallons water) and Trisodium Phosphate (1 cup TSP per 5 gallons water). After soaking, take the cartridge out of the water and scrub it in fresh water. Do not use soap; it makes the water sudsy.

3 **Reassembling the Filter.** Examine the cartridge before reassembling the filter. If the fabric does not come clean, or if it has begun to deteriorate or tear, or it appears shiny and closed, replace it. Reassemble the filter and resume normal operation. With the pump operating, open the relief valve until water squirts out; this allows trapped air to escape.

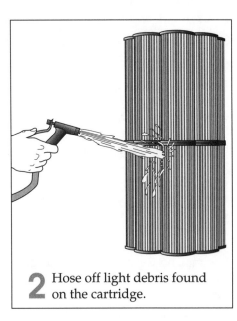

2 Hose off light debris found on the cartridge.

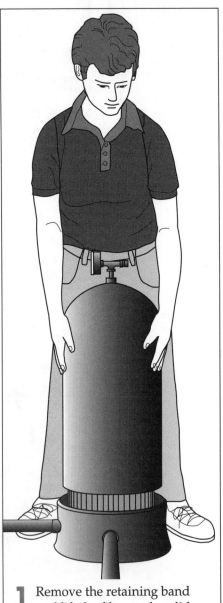

1 Remove the retaining band and lift the filter tank or lid from the base.

3 Examine the cartridge before reassembling the filter. If it is torn or worn, replace it.

HEATERS

By heating the pool just a few hours each day, you can extend the swimming season several weeks into the spring and fall. In warmer climates, a heater can allow you to swim all year round. Modern pool heaters controlled by solid-state technology are energy efficient. In other words, you will not have to take out a second mortgage just to heat the pool.

Pool System Heaters

Unlike a traditional household water heater, a pool heater does not have a large reservoir of preheated water. Water is heated as it passes through the heater's copper coils creating a mixture of heated and cold water. The water that exits from the heater is not more than 10 to 25 degrees warmer than the water that entered.

The basic principle is simple: A burner (similar to a gas burner or electric element on a stove top) creates heat. The heat rises in the heater's cabinet to the coils located above. Water passes through the heated coils and is returned to the pool. Because the heating demands are low, solar pool heaters, which offer free heat without complicated hardware, are a viable alternative to gas and electric heaters in many parts of the country.

Gas Heater Safety

Because a pool heater combines combustible fuel, pressurized water, and electricity, working on one requires extra safety considerations:

■ Do not attempt to repair safety controls and combination gas valves. Always replace them. A failure to repair them correctly could be disastrous. When in doubt, call a professional pool technician.

■ Never strike a gas valve or other heating component in an attempt to make it operate.

■ Keep wiring away from the sharp metal edges of the heater as well as all hot areas.

■ Make sure everyone knows the heater is under repair to avoid accidental ignition.

■ When attempting to fire a heater, keep your face and body away from the heater tray. Accumulated gas vapors can ignite out-ward instantly, especially if you are using a propane (LP)-fueled unit.

Gas-Fueled Heaters

Water enters a gas-fueled heater through copper exchanger tubes located above a burner tray. Because of the excellent heat conductivity of copper, heat rising from the burner tray transfers efficiently to the water in the exchanger. On most heaters, water goes through at least four of the tubes and picks up 6 to 9 degrees on each pass before leaving the heater. Gas-fueled heaters are divided into two categories based on the type of pilot and the method of ignition.

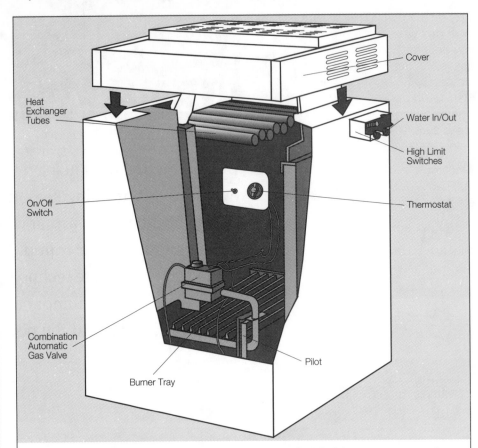

Gas-Fueled Heaters. Gas-fueled heaters are divided into two categories: standing pilot and electronic pilot units.

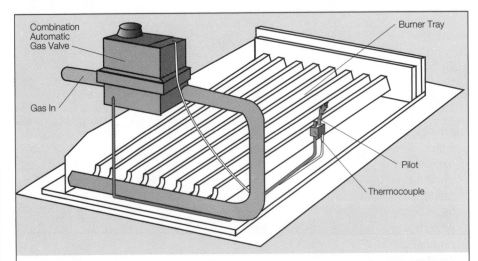

Millivolt or Standing Pilot Heaters. The temperature of a pilot flame may be more than 1,100°F. Be careful when working nearby.

Millivolt or Standing Pilot Heaters.
This type of heater has a pilot that is constantly lit. A thermocouple converts the heat that comes from the pilot into electricity, powering a number of control switches. Together, the control switches constitute a control circuit. When electricity passes through the entire control circuit, the main gas valve opens and the burner tray becomes flooded with gas. The gas is then ignited by the pilot. The temperature of a pilot flame is more than 1,100 degrees F. Be careful when working near a pilot assembly. Make sure it has been off for a while before beginning work.

Electronic Pilot Heaters. A heater that has an electronic ignition uses an electric spark to ignite gas in a burner tray. This is the only difference between it and a millivolt or standing pilot gas heater. The voltage for the pilot spark travels from a 110-volt (or 220-volt) utility line to a 24-volt transformer, and then into a switching device called the intermittent ignition device (IID). From the IID, the current follows a path through the control circuit switches. After enough electricity flows through the control circuit, the current returns to the IID, sending a charge along a special wire to the pilot ignition electrode. The IID then opens the gas line to the burner tray (which becomes flooded with gas), igniting it with the pilot flame.

Electric Heaters

Electric heaters, which are used primarily for spas, are usually smaller than gas heaters. Normally, they are not used for pools except in places where gas is unavailable. This is due to their slower heating time, a high cost of operation, and the high amps and heavy wiring they require. A typical electric heater has many similar components as a gas heater except that the heat comes from an electric coil that is immersed in water as it passes through the unit. There is no open flame as with gas heaters.

Small tube-shaped units sometimes are used in small portable spas. These units often do not have control circuits, but may have a simple mechanical thermostat control. This is because the other controls are built into the spa's control panel.

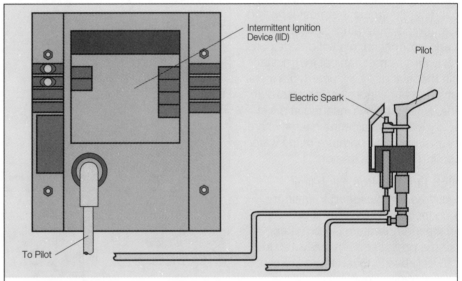

Electronic Pilot Heaters. This type of heater uses an electric spark to ignite gas in the burner tray.

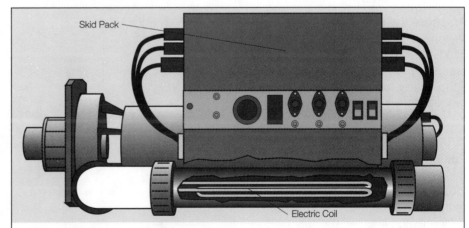

Electric Heaters. Heat comes from an electric coil that is immersed in the water as it passes through the unit.

Natural vs. Propane Gas

There are differences between these two types of heating fuels. Both natural gas and propane (LP) must be treated with great respect and all safety procedures strictly abided. Since it is lighter than air, natural gas tends to dissipate quickly if it is not ignited immediately. It has a distinctive odor which acts as a warning of its presence. Propane, on the other hand, is heavier than air so when it floods the burner tray and is not ignited, it sits on the bottom of the heater. Since it does not float upward, chances are you may not smell it either. If it suddenly ignites, the explosion will be directed out toward the front panel of the heater. Therefore never put your face close up to the front panel while trying to figure out why the heater has not started up. Follow safety guidelines and never get careless around propane.

Control Circuits

The control circuit is comprised of a series of safety switches that test the heater for various conditions before allowing electricity to pass on to the main gas valve and fire up the unit. Understanding the components in the circuit is essential to maintaining and repairing a heater.

On/Off Switch. The on/off switch usually is a simple toggle-type switch located on the heater next to the thermostat control. The switch also can be remotely located, allowing you to turn it on or off from a more convenient location.

Thermostat. Thermostats fall into two categories: electronic and mechanical. The electronic thermostat has an electronic temperature sensor that feeds information to a solid-state control board. A mechanical thermostat is a rheostat dial connected to a metal tube that ends in a slender metal bulb. The oil-filled bulb is inserted in a wet or dry location inside the heater where it senses the temperature of the water coming out of the heater.

High-Limit Switch. High-limit switches are designed to maintain a connection in the circuit as long as their temperature does not exceed a preset limit—usually 120 to 150 degrees F. Often there are two on the same circuit. While the fusible link detects high air temperature, the high-limit switch detects high water temperatures.

Pressure Switch. This is a simple switching device located at the end of a hollow metal tube that ensures enough water is getting to the heater. If the heater runs low on water, it means there is not enough pressure to close the switch, so the circuit breaks and the heater shuts down.

Fusible Link. Some heaters use a fusible link; a heat-sensitive device located on a ceramic holder in front of the gas burner tray. If the heat becomes too intense, the link melts and breaks the circuit. This occurs if debris catches fire on the tray itself

or if part of the burner is rusted out and therefore causes high flames. The link also melts if improper venting occurs or if low gas pressure causes the flame from the burner tray to roll in the link's direction.

Automatic Gas Valve. The automatic gas valve often is called the combination gas valve because it combines the main burner tray gas valve and a separately activated pilot gas valve. The components of the control circuit work together to start the electric flow at the main gas valve, which releases gas to flood the burner tray. The pilot then ignites the gas and the heater burns until the

control circuit is broken for some reason. The circuit may break for the following reasons:

- The desired temperature is reached and the thermostat switch opens.

- The water pressure drops inside the heater (such as when the pump is turned off) and the pressure switch opens.

- The heater is turned off at the on/off switch.

- Air or water temperature exceeds set limits and the fusible link or high-limit switches open.

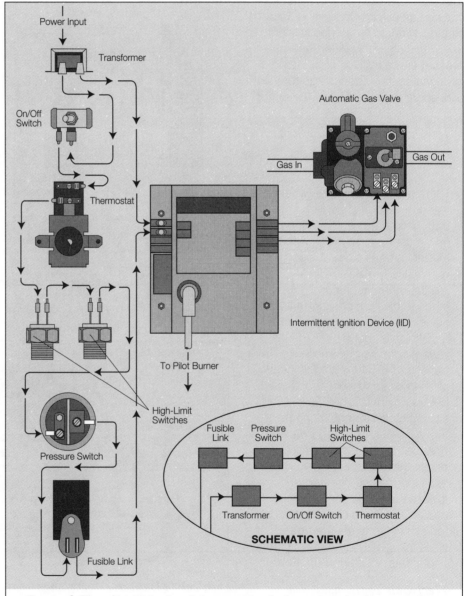

Control Circuits. This circuit is comprised of a series of safety switches.

Heater Repairs & Maintenance

The most important concern when working on heater repairs or adjustments is safety. Take your time, and follow all recommended precautions. The actual troubleshooting and repair of a heater is not difficult. Control circuit component repairs are most common.

Disassembling the Control Circuit

Understanding the components of the control circuit is essential to heater repair, but more important is locating exactly where a failure is and fixing that specific element. If the heater is not firing, the best way to detect the problem is to follow the path of the electricity. Use a multimeter (available at local electronics stores) to check that the electricity is reaching and leaving each switch. If not, the switch may be faulty.

All the wires for the components simply unclip or easily come off by loosening a screw. Removing a faulty switch is no problem. The hard part is determining which switch is faulty and why it is not working.

Locating the Fault in a Circuit

Electronic Ignition Heater. If the pool has an electronic ignition heater, make sure that 25 volts are leaving the transformer. Set the multimeter at 50 volts alternating current (AC). Touch the negative lead of the meter to the neutral side of the transformer, and the positive lead to the hot side. Next, leave the negative lead touching the neutral on the transformer, and touch the positive lead to each switch of the circuit until the location of the one that has no current becomes apparent. This is where the circuit is broken and the problem exists. Follow the same procedure for electric heaters that use the same control circuit. The only difference is that the voltage in the circuit will be the same as the incoming utility voltage (120 or 220 volts), so set the meter accordingly.

Standing Pilot Heaters. Follow the same procedure as just stated. Check the beginning of the circuit to see whether the pilot generator is delivering 400 to 700 millivolts. Set the meter to 1 volt direct current (DC), and touch the negative lead of the meter to the negative terminal on the gas valve. Then set the positive lead to the positive terminal. Leave the negative lead touching the negative terminal on the gas valve, and move the positive lead around the circuit. Continue to check each switch as instructed until the break in the circuit is located.

Solving Other Circuit Problems

Pressure Switch. The pressure switch opens (shuts off) when water circulation is obstructed. Obstructions are caused by a clogged skimmer basket or main drain, a clogged pump strainer basket, a dirty filter, or low water levels in the pool or spa. Check all of these before touching the pressure switch itself. The pressure switch unscrews from the end of the water tube that feeds it.

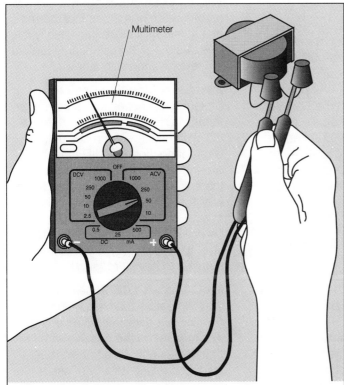

Electronic Ignition Heater. Use a multimeter to make sure 25 volts leave the transformer.

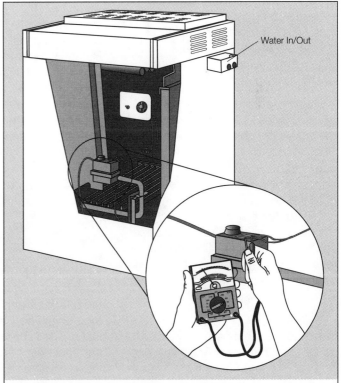

Standing Pilot Heaters. Use a multimeter to make sure the pilot generator is delivering 400 to 700 millivolts.

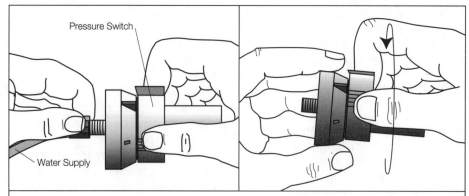

Pressure Switch. Unscrew the pressure switch from the water supply tube (left). These adjustments are very sensitive so be sure to turn the knob just one-quarter turn each time (right).

If the water is circulating adequately, it may not be reaching the pressure switch. Turn off the heater (at the on/off switch), turn off the electricity to the pump, remove the wires to the switch, and unscrew the switch from the water supply tube. Then turn on the pump. If water flows strongly out of the tube, check the hole at the end of the pressure switch to make sure it is clean. If the switch is rusted, leaking or cannot be cleaned, replace it.

If water does not come out of the tube, call a professional pool technician. The repair requires taking off the top of the heater vent and disassembling many of the heat exchanger components.

Adjust the pressure switch so that it is more or less sensitive by turning the screw or knob on the switch. Some units have a nut that holds the screw in place. Others have a spring on the screw that provides tension to hold the adjustment. Tightening the screw (or knob on some models) makes the switch more pressure sensitive, so the heater will come on with less pressure. Loosening the screw or knob makes the switch less pressure sensitive, so the heater will come on with more pressure.

These adjustments are very sensitive, so be sure to turn the knob only one quarter of a turn each time. Check the operation after each small turn until the heater properly operates. When circulating properly, the heater

will fire and stay lit. It will stop within five seconds after circulation stops.

Fusible Link. Often overheating, usually caused by poor ventilation, causes fusible links to fail. The fusible link is held in place by a ceramic holder. After replacing a fusible link, check the heater for leaves or anything else that might surround the cabinet and restrict the air flow.

High-Limit Switch. High-limit switches differ from heater to heater, but the principles are the same. Some heaters have two high-limit switches located side-by-side and beneath a small protective cover. Remove the cover and pull the switches and their retainer bracket from the header area (the pump can be left on or off). Then pull (or unscrew, depending on the model) the switches from the bracket and replace them. It is a good idea to replace both switches at this time; if one has worn out, the other may not be far behind.

In other heaters, the switches are located on each side of the heat exchanger. Turn off the pump. Follow the wiring to the switch, pull off the wires, and unscrew the switch from the header. Put pipe dope or Teflon tape on the new switch to prevent leaks. Then screw it into the header and reconnect the wires. Because these switches are located on opposite sides of the heat exchanger, they are heated at different rates and, therefore, wear out at different

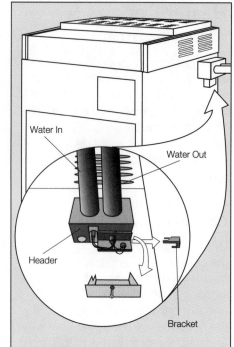

High-Limit Switch. The high-limit switches are located beneath a small protective cover.

rates—so it is not necessary to replace both if one fails.

On/Off Switch and Thermostat. Very little can go wrong with a simple on/off switch or mechanical thermostat. If either of these fail, usually it is due to old age or rust. Simply replace the faulty switch with a new one.

Intermittent Ignition Device. Although it is not exactly a computer, the IID is quite sophisticated. Most IID problems are the result of loose wire connections. An IID must be grounded in order to operate, so if there is a problem, check the ground wire first. The wires must be free from corrosion and the connections must be solid. Although they are expensive, it is less costly to buy a new IID than it is to have it repaired.

Problems with the Fuses. Some 24-volt heaters have an in-line fuse (similar to a car radio fuse) located in a bracket on the positive wire that comes out of the transformer. Inspect the fuse visually or use a multimeter to check if a current exits the fuse.

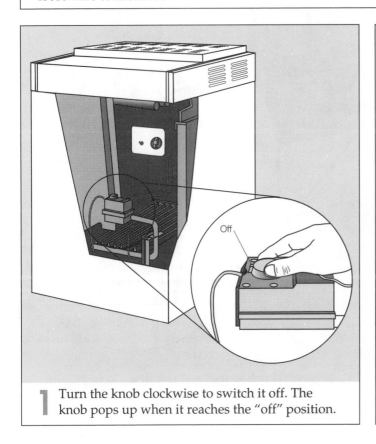

Intermittent Ignition Device. Most IID problems are the result of loose wire connections.

Lighting or Relighting the Pilot Flame

The most frequent task required by a standing pilot-type heater is lighting the pilot flame. Look for lighting instructions on the heater itself and follow them.

Note: The procedure below is for millivolt heaters only. The pilot burner in electronic ignition heaters lights automatically with an electronic spark. The following is the most common procedure:

1 Turning Off the Heater. Turn the combination gas valve control knob to the "off" position. To be safe, wait five minutes until all the gas in the burner tray and around the pilot is gone. Turn the on/off switch to "off".

2 Lighting the Pilot Burner. Turn the control knob to "pilot" and push it down (on some models the knob is pushed down half-way before turning, then all the way down when it reaches "pilot"). The gas makes a hissing sound from the end of the pilot. If there is no sound, the pilot may be clogged with insects or rust.

1 Turn the knob clockwise to switch it off. The knob pops up when it reaches the "off" position.

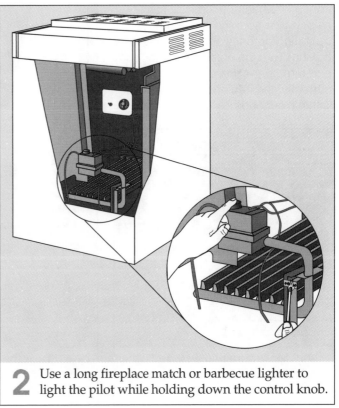

2 Use a long fireplace match or barbecue lighter to light the pilot while holding down the control knob.

Use a long fireplace match or barbecue lighter to light the pilot while continuing to hold down the control knob. If the heater has a pilot lighting tube, hold the match in front of the tube to light the pilot burner. Some pilot lighting tubes have their own gas supply, so light the tube as soon as the control knob is depressed.

Hold down the control for at least a minute (so heat from the pilot generates enough electricity in the thermocouple to power the gas valve). The pilot gas valve opens automatically after that, and the control circuit opens the main burner gas valve. Release the control and the pilot will remain lit.

3 **Verifying the Pilot Flame.** A strong blue flame of 2 to 3 inches extends towards the burner tray, while another flame of equal proportions heats the thermocouple. Make sure the pilot is securely in place and close enough to the burner tray to quickly ignite the main burner.

4 **Firing the Heater.** Turn the gas valve control knob to the "on" position, and stand back and to one side of the heater. Never stand in front of the heater in case of flashback. Make sure the pool pump is operating properly and that water is flowing. Turn the on/off switch to "on" and turn up the thermostat. If done correctly, the heater usually fires within 6 seconds.

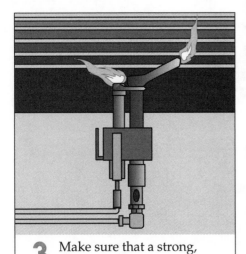

3 Make sure that a strong, 2- to 3-in. blue flame extends toward the burner tray.

Preventive Maintenance

The best way to maintain a heater is to use it regularly. It is far more economical to keep the heater going for a short time every day during the swimming season, than to turn it up high just on the days that the pool is being used. The heat generated from regular use prevents corrosion by drying rust-causing moisture; discourages insects and rodents from nesting; and keeps electricity flowing through all the circuits. The heat also burns off wind-borne leaves and debris that land in the top vents. An accumulation of leaves and debris is a fire hazard.

Visually inspect the heater on a regular basis to detect sooting, water or gas leaks, and other problems before they get out of hand. Keep the top of the heater clean and free from dirt and debris. Make sure the pilot and burner flames are strong, blue, and at least 2 to 3 inches in height. Open the drain plug on the heat exchanger and check for scale buildup.

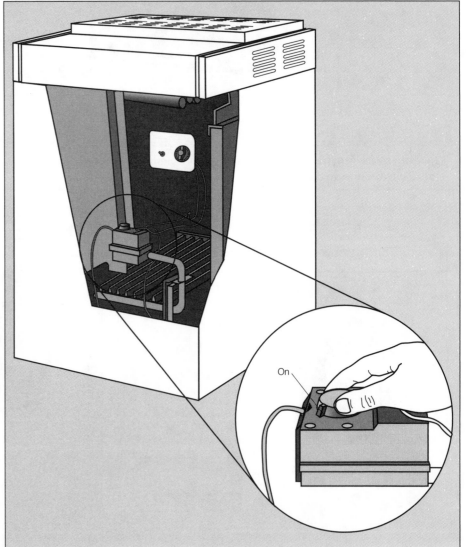

4 Turn the gas valve control knob to the "on" position.

CLEANING A POOL OR SPA

Keeping your pool or spa clean is vital to healthy use and enjoyment. Some jobs, such as skimming the pool, must be done daily during the swimming season. Other jobs, such as vacuuming, need to be done on a weekly basis. Cleaning the pool helps the chemicals in the water work effectively.

General Cleaning Procedures

When cleaning the pool, follow the same path the water takes as it passes through the circulation system. First skim the water to remove leaves and debris. Then use tile soap to scrub the tiles clean. Next, clean the skimmer basket, and then shut off the pump and clean the pump strainer basket. Reprime the pump and check for correct filter pressure. If the filter pressure is high, the filter may be dirty and require backwashing (see page 36). Thoroughly brush the pool. Vacuum the pool, test the water chemistry, and add the necessary chemicals. After the pool cleaning is done, it is a good idea to clean the decking and the area around the pool. Debris, leaves, and dirt around the pool eventually find their way into the water.

Skimming the Surface

Cleaning begins at the surface of the water. It is easier to get rid of floating debris, than it is to dispose of debris that has settled to the bottom. Use a telepole and leaf rake to remove all floating debris from the surface. When the net is full, empty it into a trash can or plastic garbage bag. Do not empty the net into the yard or garden, because as soon as the debris dries, it will blow back into the pool.

Scraping the Tile Line. When skimming, be sure to scrape along the tile line. Tile attracts small bits of leaves and dirt. Make sure the leaf rake has a rubber or plastic edge so it does not scratch the tile.

Cleaning Tile

There is good reason to clean the tile before vacuuming. Dirt falls from the tiles as they are being cleaned and settles to the bottom of the pool. Also, if stubborn stains need to be removed with a pumice stone, bits of the stone break off and end up on the bottom of the pool.

Use a tile brush and tile soap to clean the tiles. Tile soap is sold at pool supply stores. To provide extra strength for cutting stubborn stains and oils, mix one part muriatic acid to five parts soap. Use soap that is specifically designed for pool tiles. Other types of soap foam up when they get into the circulation system.

Evaporation and refilling cause the waterline to change, so be sure to

Skimming the Surface. Use a telepole and leaf rake to skim debris from the surface of the water.

Scraping the Tile Line. Scrape along the tile line to remove small bits of leaves and dirt.

Cleaning Tile. Scrub below the waterline, but be careful not to scratch the tiles.

scrub below the waterline. To prevent scratching the tiles, do not use abrasive brushes or scouring pads. Also, this is a good time to check for cracked seams in tile and coping that may have to be replaced. Faulty coping has hollow sound when tapped with a blunt instrument.

Vacuuming

There are two ways to clean a pool or spa. If the pool has only a light covering of dirt, it can be vacuumed into the pool's filter. In this case, a vacuum head and hose work off the pool system. For more significant debris, however, use a leaf vacuum (which operates on garden hose water pressure) to force debris into the bag. When the bag is full, remove and empty it.

1 **Preparing the Vacuum.** Make sure the circulation system is running normally and that there is adequate suction at the skimmer. If suction is weak, check the pump strainer pot to make sure it is not clogged with debris. Attach the vacuum head with hose to the telepole. Work near the skimmer and feed the head straight into the pool with the hose following. By slowly feeding the hose straight down, water fills it and pushes out the air. Once the entire hose is in the pool, water appears at the end you are holding.

2 **Starting Suction in the Vacuum.** Keep the hose near water level so water does not drain from it, and slide it through the weir opening into the skimmer. A hole in the bottom of the skimmer creates suction when the pump is running. Some skimmers have a second hole plumbed to the main drain, but it does not have suction. Insert the hose cuff in the suction port of the skimmer. By doing so, the vacuum head will have suction.

3 **Vacuuming the Pool.** Work around the bottom and the sides. If the pool is dirty, the places

Skimmer Cover

Skimmer

Vacuum Head

1 Work near the skimmer and feed the head straight into the pool.

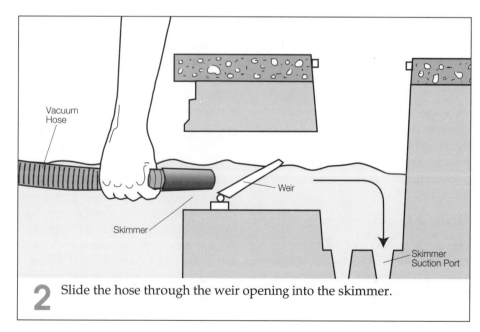

Vacuum Hose

Weir

Skimmer

Skimmer Suction Port

2 Slide the hose through the weir opening into the skimmer.

3 Vacuum the bottom and sides of the pool.

■ If the pool is very dirty, the strainer basket or filter may become filled. If the suction becomes weak, stop vacuuming and empty the pump strainer basket or clean the filter. In any case, when the vacuuming is done, inspect the pump strainer basket and filter to check if they have become clogged.

■ When vacuuming a spa that operates on the same circulation system as the swimming pool, simply lift the vacuum out of the pool and immediately place it in the spa. Do this quickly, because while the vacuum is out of the water, air enters the hose, causing it temporarily to lose suction. There should be enough water in the line for the vacuum to reprime itself. You will know the system has regained suction when bubbles are seen coming out of the return ports and the vacuum picks up debris.

Note: Usually adjacent spas have pool return lines, so the water falls from one to the other. If they do not circulate together (if both systems operate on the same circulation system by changing valve positions), the pool and spa have to be vacuumed separately. This way, the water is replaced to each system.

already vacuumed are apparent. Do not move the vacuum head too quickly. If the suction is so strong that the vacuum head sticks to the bottom of the pool, adjust the skimmer valves to adjust the flow. An option to this is to lower the wheels on the vacuum head itself, so the vacuum head raises. If suction is weak, raise the wheels so that the vacuum head lays closer to the surface, or simply vacuum at a slower pace.

After vacuuming, stand near the skimmer, and pull the hose out of the skimmer suction port. Now take the vacuum head out of the water. Suction quickly pulls the water from the hose.

Using a Leaf Vacuum

Use a leaf vacuum when there are many leaves or other larger debris in the pool. One problem with the leaf vacuum is that its effectiveness is dependent on water pressure from

a garden hose. If the water pressure is weak, the suction will be weak. Weak suction also means that as the bag becomes heavy, it may tip over, scrape the pool floor, and stir up debris or become tangled with the hose. Solve this problem simply by placing a tennis ball in the bag. The floating ball keeps the bag upright.

1 **Setting up the Leaf Vacuum.** Attach a garden hose to the leaf vacuum and clip the leaf vacuum to the telepole.

2 **Vacuuming the Pool.** Place the leaf vacuum in the pool and turn on the water from the garden hose. This is how suction is created. Vacuum the leaves and debris from the pool. Because the leaf vacuum is so large, it does the job in half the time it takes a pool system vacuum to do the same job. Do not move the leaf vacuum too fast as doing so stirs up debris. If the garden hose does not float, prevent it from stirring up de-

bris by working in such a way that the hose remains behind you.

3 **Removing the Leaf Vacuum.** To remove the leaf vacuum, turn it slightly to one side and slowly lift it through the water to the surface. If pulled straight up, some of the debris is forced out of the bag and back into the pool. For the same reason, do not turn off the water before taking the leaf vacuum out of the pool. Once the leaf vacuum is

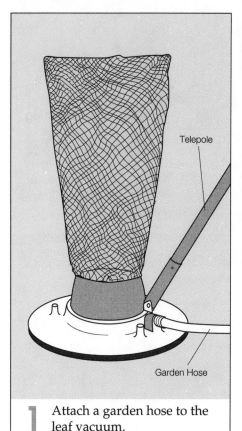

Telepole

Garden Hose

1 Attach a garden hose to the leaf vacuum.

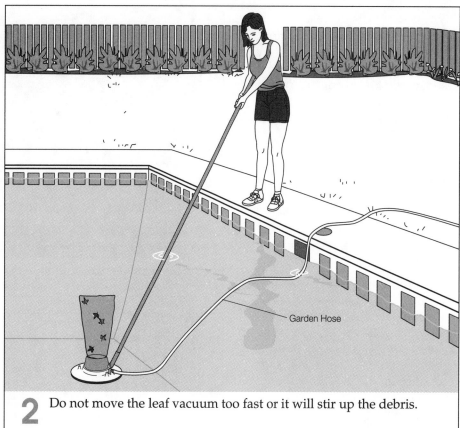

Garden Hose

2 Do not move the leaf vacuum too fast or it will stir up the debris.

on the deck, turn off the water and clean the collection bag.

Spa & Hot Tub Maintenance

Spas require some of the same chemical balance, maintenance, and cleaning that pools require, but because of the concentrated nature of spas, it usually is easier to drain a spa (rather than spend hours trying to rebalance the chemistry or clean the shell while the water is still in it).

The chemicals added to spa water must be more exact than those added to a pool. Plastic spas are not made with an alkaline material that counteracts acidic water (often caused by urine and body acids). Acidic water is more damaging in a spa because the heat of the water accelerates the destruction of the interior surfaces of metal pool equipment. Be precise when balancing spa chemistry, especially when dealing with pH.

3 To avoid dropping the debris out of the collection bag, remove the leaf vacuum at an angle.

Cleaning a Spa

1 Draining the Spa. Before draining a spa, turn off the pump and remove trippers from the time clock. Use a portable submersible pump to drain the spa. The cord is waterproof and the pump activates when plugged into a standard household outlet. Attach the vacuum hose to the pump's discharge pipe and lower the pump into the deepest part of the spa. Drape the hose out of the spa and direct the water to a waste drain. If the spa is located indoors, direct the waste water to a deep sink or bathtub drain.

2 Scrubbing the Spa. A submersible pump does not run dry and burn out because it retains the last inch of water and circulates it to keep the pump cool. As the spa is being scrubbed, leave the pump on to discard the dirty, soapy water. Do not use abrasive cleansers or pads to clean the spa—they scratch the surface. Instead, use a soft-bristle brush or sponge and a non-foaming soap, such as pool tile soap or products specially designed for spa cleaning. Scrub out the spa, tile (if any), and the opening of the skimmer. Empty debris from the skimmer basket. Rinse the spa thoroughly to remove soap residue (even non-foaming soap can cause some foaming).

3 Refilling and Restarting the Spa. Remove the pump and refill the spa with water. While the spa is filling, there is time to clean the filter and the pump strainer pot. When the spa is full, reprime the pump and adjust the spa chemistry to the proper levels.

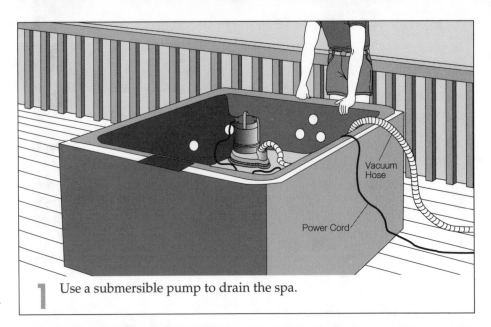

1 Use a submersible pump to drain the spa.

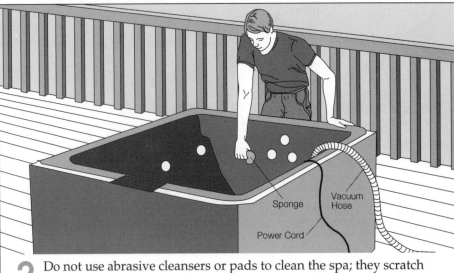

2 Do not use abrasive cleansers or pads to clean the spa; they scratch the surface.

3 Clean the filter and pump strainer pot while the spa is being filled.

POOL ACCESSORIES & EQUIPMENT

The pleasure of owning a pool is enhanced by accessories such as a time clock for automated functions, a diving board for play, lighting for night swimming, and a slide for the kids. These accessories make the most of a pool, but they also require some basic maintenance and repair.

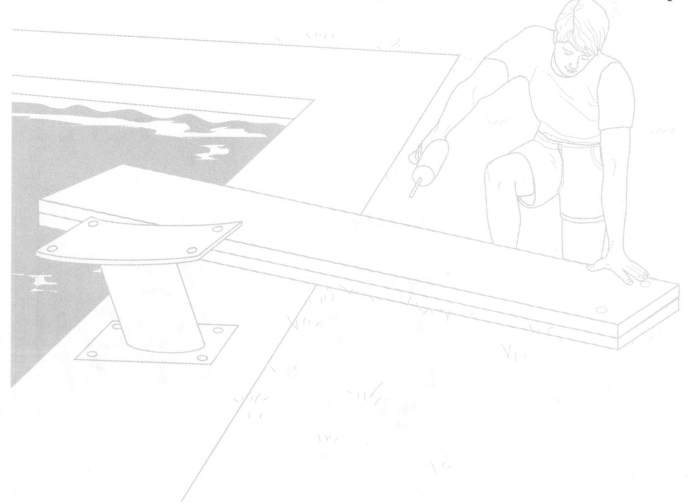

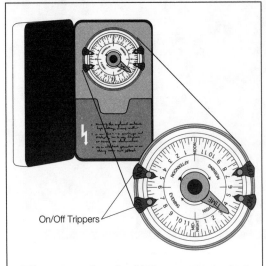

Electromechanical Timers. Time clocks allow many different on/off settings during a 24-hour day.

On/Off Trippers

Twist Timers. These are used mostly with booster motors and blowers on spas.

OFF
10
20
30
40
50
60
TURN PAST 10 THEN SET TIME

Time Clocks

A time clock can be a key component to a pool or spa. It automatically turns the pool's machinery on and off. With a time clock, the pump circulates water, the filter cleans the pool, and the heater warms the water automatically. Clocks also can be used for other things such as turning on decorative lights and fountains.

Electromechanical Timers. Time clocks are run by small electric motors and allow for many on/off settings during a 24-hour day. The pool time clock is different from other time clocks in that it has only one hand, and that hand remains still while the clock face rotates. Each appliance requires its own clock. For example, if you want to run the pump during the day and activate the pool lights at night, two clocks are needed.

On and off trippers are used to set the clock. The words "on" and "off" are labeled on the trippers. Set them for the desired times, and the clock will control the flow of electricity to a specific piece of machinery. Screw terminals are located at the bottom of the clock so it can be attached to the wires of the appliance (motor, light fixture, etc.). Electricity flows into the clock from a household circuit breaker.

Twist Timers. Twist timers are used mostly with booster motors. They are also used for blowers on spas. Whatever the twist timer is controlling will remain on for the time period set. The mechanical timer is spring loaded to unwind the minutes selected. Once the spring unwinds, the circuit breaks and shuts off the appliance. A twist timer fits into a typical light-switch box and does not contain serviceable parts. The faceplate usually shows 15, 30, 45, and 60 minutes.

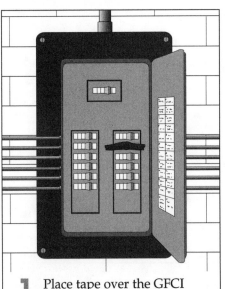

1 Place tape over the GFCI breaker so no one turns it back on while you are working.

Twist timers are handy and safe because there is no way to forget to turn them off. This is important in a spa, where people often do not realize how much time has passed, and would stay in the spa for too long if not for the timer. Twist timers also are good for controlling lighting that is not meant to be left on all night.

Time Clock Replacement

Time clocks are too inexpensive to bother fixing. If a time clock fails, simply buy a new one. When replacing a unit, make sure it has the same voltage as the original clock. If the clock is to sit in a waterproof box, buy the same brand to ensure a correct fit.

1 **Shutting off the Electricity.** Always turn off the electricity at the breaker. Place tape over the GFCI breaker so no one accidentally switches it back on while you are working.

2 **Disconnecting the Old Clock.** Remove the "load" wires, the "line" wires, and the ground wire from the old clock. Use tape to label each wire for easy reconnections.

3 **Replacing the Clock.** Unscrew or unclip the existing clock from the box and snap or screw the new one in place. Reattach the wires. If

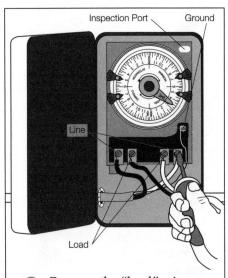

Inspection Port   Ground

Line

Load

2 Remove the "load" wires, the "line" wires, and the ground wire.

3 Snap or screw the new time clock in place.

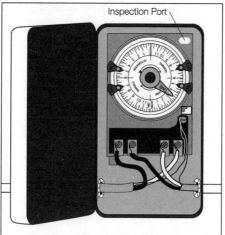

Inspection Port

4 View the clock gears through the visual inspection port.

the new clock is not configured exactly like the old one, make sure that the electrical supply wires attach to the "line" terminals of the clock. The two appliance wires from the pool equipment attach to the "load" terminals. The electrical cable will have a black hot wire, a white neutral wire, and a bare ground wire. If line and load is not marked, look for the screws where the clock motor is connected. The two internal clock wires always are attached to the "line" terminals.

4 **Testing the Clock.** Turn on the power and test the clock by turning the manual on/off lever to "on." Make sure that the power going to the time clock is not switch operated

(it may accidentally be switched off sometime and then, when it is switched on again, the time will be wrong). Most clocks have a visual inspection opening, so the user can see if the clock is operating.

Diving Boards

As diving boards age they can become dangerous and must be replaced. The signs of age include a warped surface, visible cracks,

and a crackling sound when the board is used. Diving boards are made out of wood for flexibility, covered with fiberglass to make them waterproof, and topped with a non-skid tread. They are available in spring-assisted and simple platform models. Most boards for home use are 6 to 12 feet long and 18 inches wide. When replacing a board, buy the same type and length as the original.

To accommodate even the smallest diving board, a pool must be at least 7½ feet deep, 15 feet wide, and 28 feet long.

Note: *Before buying a board, check the local codes in your area.*

If the fiberglass cover cracks or delaminates, it may cause the board's wooden interior to rot. A cracked board cannot be cosmetically repaired; there is a danger that it may snap in two.

The sun can destroy the nonskid material on top of the board. Replacing this material is the only repair that can be made safely to a diving board. Buy a tread kit and follow manufacturer's instructions.

Lubricating a Time Clock

Turn off the power at the main service box and remove the clock from the box as described on page 56. Leave the wires attached. Expose the back of the clock and spray penetrating oil lubricant around the gears. Next, spray the lubricant on the gears behind the dial face. Do not get the lubricant on the electrical contacts. Place the clock into the box and turn on the power. Turn the clock on and off a few times to work in the lube.

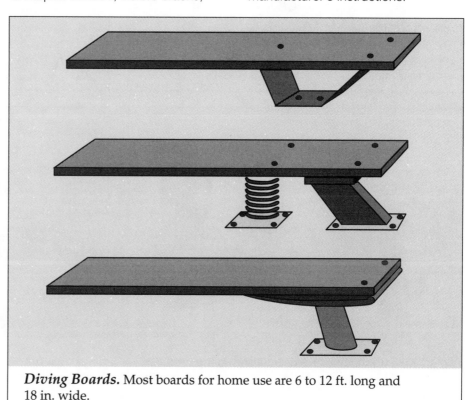

Diving Boards. Most boards for home use are 6 to 12 ft. long and 18 in. wide.

Replacing a Diving Board

1 Unfastening the Old Board.
Counterbalance the board before removing its fasteners. Usually 20 pounds of weight is enough (or have a helper sit on the end of the board) to keep it from dropping into the pool. Remove the nuts, lock washers, flat washers, and the bolt plates from the mounting hardware that holds the board to the stand.

2 Removing the Old Board.
Take the board off the stand. Use a helper to do this; boards are heavier than they look, especially waterlogged boards.

3 Preparing the New Board.
Lay the new board on the pool deck. Place the old board on top of the new one and use it as a template for drilling bolt holes in the new board. Place scrap wood (a 2x4 works well) under the end being drilled to avoid drilling into the pool deck. Use a standard power drill and drill bit to make the holes. The bit must be no more than 1/16 inch larger than the diameter of the bolt. Some stands have a rubber cushion that also might need to be replaced. New replacement boards come with cushions. Simply lift off the old cushion and lay the new one in place. Most stands also have a rubber gasket on the bolted end. Replace this gasket as well.

4 Installing the New Board.
Place the new board on the stand, using the counterweight until it is secured. Put the bolt plate on the new board and insert the bolts. No matter how good the old ones look, use the new bolts that come with the new board. On the underside of the board, replace the nuts, lock washers, flat washers, and bolt plates with the ones that come with the new board. If lock washers do not come with the new board, buy them sepa-

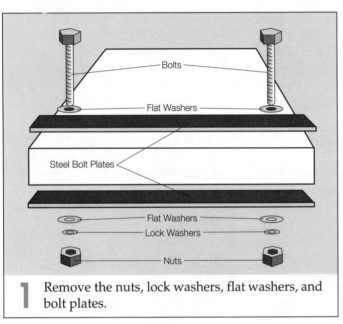

1 Remove the nuts, lock washers, flat washers, and bolt plates.

Labels: Bolts, Flat Washers, Steel Bolt Plates, Flat Washers, Lock Washers, Nuts

2 A diving board is heavier than it looks, especially one that is waterlogged.

3 Line up the two boards (old one on top) and use the old board as a pattern for drilling holes in the new one.

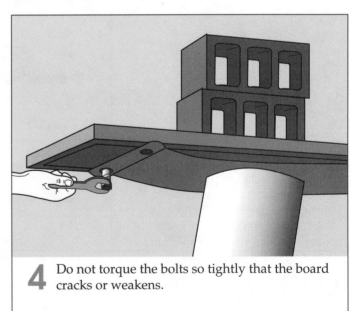

4 Do not torque the bolts so tightly that the board cracks or weakens.

rately and install them; they prevent the nuts from loosening over time. Never tighten a nut unless it is accompanied by washers and a bolt plate. Jumping on the board places great stress on the nuts, and without washers or the bolt plate to distribute the stress evenly, the nut might tear through the board. Do not torque the bolts so tightly that the board cracks or weakens. Be sure the board is aligned with its fulcrum or it will twist and become seriously weakened.

Ladders, Rails, & Slides

A good safety measure for pools that are more than 20 feet wide is to have a ladder on both sides of the deep end. Ladders must have at least two steps (approximately 24 inches) below the normal water level and handrails that are 17 to 24 inches apart to accommodate the average swimmer.

Rails are best located in the middle of the entry steps found at the shallow end. Rails must be bolted or screwed such that tools are needed for their removal.

Slides are made of fiberglass and have metal steps and frames. Straight slides are 8 to 13 feet long and use up a significant amount of space on the pool deck. Curved slides are available for decks that are limited in space. Just like diving boards, the higher the slide, the greater depth required at that location.

Replacing a Ladder, Rail, or Slide

This step-by-step project describes how to replace a rail. The directions are the same for replacing ladders and slides.

1 **Exposing the Hardware.** At the base of each leg there is a decorative cover called an escutcheon plate. Slide this plate up the rail leg to expose the mounting hardware. If the rail is cemented to the deck, pro- fessional help is necessary to cut out the old unit, drill out the legs from the concrete, and install a new unit.

2 **Removing the Old Rail.** The legs are firmly secured by a metal wedge that tightens or loosens with a bolt that is part of a mechanism. Use a flat-blade screwdriver to unscrew the bolted wedge and pry out the spring mechanism to loosen the rail leg. Loosen the leg on the deck first, then step into the pool and reach into the water to loosen the leg that is attached to the pool floor. Lift out the old rail.

3 **Installing the New Rail.** Slide the escutcheon plates onto the legs before setting the new rail in place. Make sure the plates face the

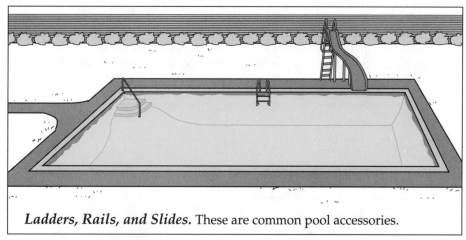

Ladders, Rails, and Slides. These are common pool accessories.

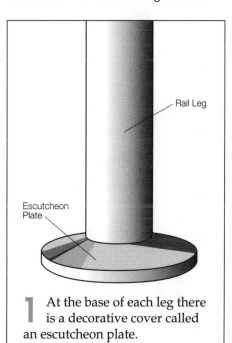

1 At the base of each leg there is a decorative cover called an escutcheon plate.

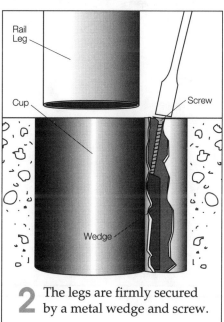

2 The legs are firmly secured by a metal wedge and screw.

3 Set the rail in the mounting cups and check for height, fit, and level.

correct direction. Set the rail in the mounting cups and check for height and fit. Tighten the mounting hardware and slide the plates onto the deck and pool floor.

Ladder, Rail, & Slide Maintenance

Ladders and rails do not require special maintenance or cleaning, but using a household metal cleaner to polish them occasionally keeps them bright. Do not use abrasive cleansers that scratch shiny metal surfaces. Slides are made of fiberglass and can discolor. A glaze or polish kit, available at pool supply stores, restores the slide's appearance. Never attempt to paint a slide.

Periodically, shake the ladder, rail, or slide to detect loose installation. Also, check for rusty bolts. If the slide has a water supply, check for leaks that can cause equipment to run dry and overheat.

Automatic Pool Cleaners

There are two types of automatic pool cleaners. A booster pump system uses the pool's circulation along with an additional integrated pump to suck up dirt and sweep debris to the skimmer and drain. The booster pump is located alongside the other pool equipment and is plumbed into the circulation system via the pipe that goes from the heater back to the pool. The other type of pool cleaner uses the pool's circulation system as the only means of suction and agitation. Both of these systems drastically cut down on time spent manually skimming and cleaning the pool.

Booster Pump Systems

Booster pump systems take water which is already on its way back to the pool (after the filter and heater) and turbocharge or further pressurize

it by running it through a separate pump or motor. This high-pressure stream of water passes through flexible hoses into a cleaner that roams the pool. There are two common types of booster pump cleaning systems: vacuum head and sweep head.

Vacuum Head. The vacuum-head cleaner has a catch bag for collecting debris. Pressurized water from the booster pump enters through the stalk (a port on the top of the cleaner). Some of the water is blasted out the tail, stirring up dirt on the pool bottom so it can be filtered by the pool's circulation system. The rest of the water powers a turbine on a horizontal shaft which turns the wheels and moves the unit forward. Some water is diverted to a thrust jet which can be adjusted up or down to keep the unit from moving nose-up. The head float keeps the unit upright.

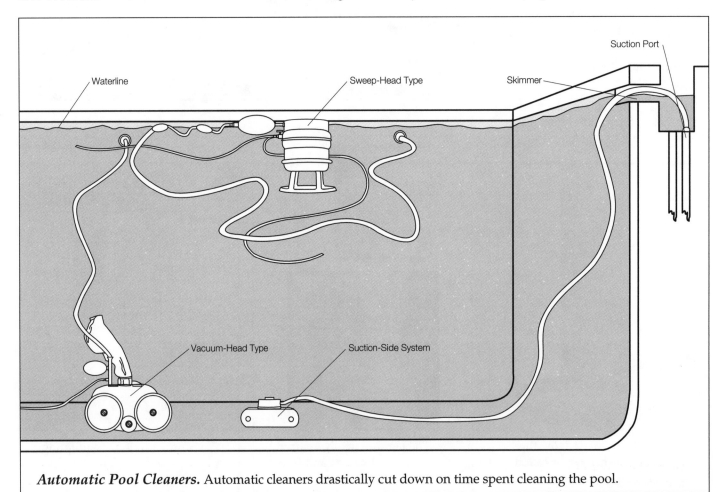

Automatic Pool Cleaners. Automatic cleaners drastically cut down on time spent cleaning the pool.

Sweep Head. The sweep-head cleaner floats on the water and has long, flexible, swirling arms that stir up debris found along the pool walls and bottom. The head floats on the water and travels around the pool by way of a bottom-mounted propeller that is fed by the booster pump. The main drain uses suction to pull the agitated debris into its basket which is removed and emptied when full. The finer dirt is caught in the filter.

Note: Never operate a booster pump system unless the circulation pump is working as well. Since the booster is not self-priming, it needs the system's circulation pump to provide water. Running it dry causes the pump to overheat and warp or burn out the seal.

Booster System Repairs & Adjustments

Repairs to cleaning systems are easy to do. The symptoms associated with potential problems are listed here:

Water Does Not Flow From Jets. Because the jets are small, they clog easily. To catch dirt particles or DE that gets through the filter, install a fine-mesh strainer at the point where the plumbing connects to the feeder hose. Sand and dirt that is picked up by the unit clogs the internal jets. This may be a sign that dirt or sand is wreaking havoc with the rest of the system as well.

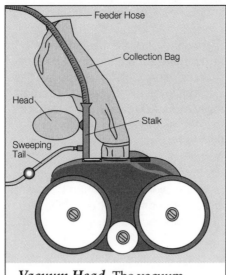

Vacuum Head. The vacuum head has a catch bag for collecting debris.

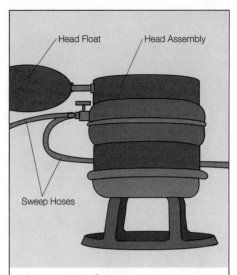

Sweep Head. The sweep head has long, flexible arms that swirl along the walls and the bottom of the pool, stirring up debris.

Vacuum Head Runs; Does Not Pick Up Debris. The water pressure supplied to the vacuum head might be too powerful for normal operation. This happens when the return pressure is very strong. Special pressure-reducing washers can be added at the vacuum hose connection. These washers are smaller in diameter than the plumbing, so they restrict the amount of water that flows to the vacuum head.

Wheels Wobble; Vacuum Head Falls. Solve this problem by replacing the wheel bearings. The wheel is held to the axle with a single plastic screw. Use your finger or a screw-

driver to pull out the old bearings. Then pop in the new ones, making sure the shielded side faces toward the outside. Worn tires must be replaced if they do not properly engage the drive wheel. Tires are easy to remove and replace; they stretch over the wheel like a large

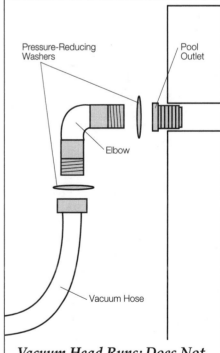

Vacuum Head Runs; Does Not Pick Up Debris. Special pressure-reducing washers are added at the vacuum hose connection.

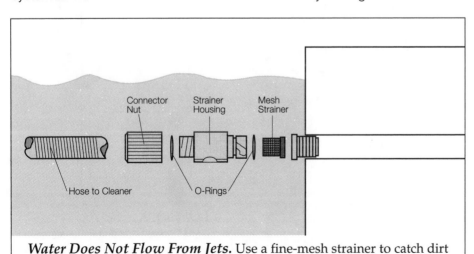

Water Does Not Flow From Jets. Use a fine-mesh strainer to catch dirt particles or DE that gets past the filter.

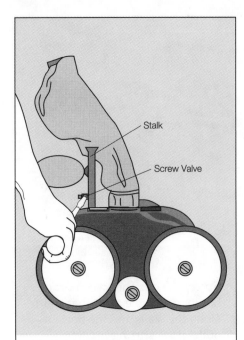

Tail Sweeps Wildly. The tail jet flow can be adjusted by tightening or loosening the screw valve.

rubber band. Do not overtighten the wheel screws; they are made of plastic and snap off easily. If the wheel screw breaks, gently tap a flat-blade screwdriver into the broken stem and remove it.

Tail Sweeps Wildly. The tail assembly is the first thing to wear out because it constantly sweeps the pool sides and bottom. If water squirts out of places in the hose where it is not supposed to, the tail will swing wildly. Rubber rings found on the tail are made to absorb wear. If the rings become worn, replace them. If the tail does not stay on the pool floor, the tail jet flow can be adjusted by tightening or loosening the screw valve that opens or closes water flow to the tail.

Suction-Side Systems

Suction-side automatic pool cleaners use the suction from the skimmer to constantly vacuum the pool. A standard vacuum hose of 1½-inch diameter connects the skimmer suction opening and the vacuum head that patrols the pool bottom.

The only trick to keeping a suction-side automatic pool cleaner func-

tioning efficiently is to keep the pump strainer pot clean. As the vacuum patrols the pool it collects leaves and other debris and sends it to the pump strainer pot. When the pot fills with obstructions, suction is dramatically reduced, causing the cleaner to become inefficient. To prevent this, keep the strainer pot clean or add a leaf collecting canister to the vacuum hose. A simple in-line canister is easier to clean than the pump strainer pot and can be purchased at a pool supply store.

Lighting

Lighting is essential if the pool is to be used at night. A typical pool or spa light is a stainless steel, cone-shaped fixture, about 8 inches in diameter and 6 to 10 inches deep. The fixture is mounted in a niche in the pool. The watertight niche simply is a metal can cemented into the

Electricity & Water

Electricity and water can be a deadly combination. Always follow all safety procedures to the letter, no matter how many times the job has to be done. An electrified pool can be the direct result of a job done carelessly.

- If a fixture, gasket, or lens looks old or worn, replace it.

- Always use a replacement lens, bulb, or gasket made specifically for the fixture. Use the same manufacturer or a generic brand designed for the specific make and model. Forcing a different part to fit invites tragedy.

- Each fixture is designed to take a specific bulb. If the writing on the bulb is not readable, never replace the bulb with one that is higher than 400 watts. Heat can melt the resin that makes the fixture waterproof.

side of the pool. A waterproof conduit travels away from the niche to the above-ground junction box (also called a J-box).

Pool lights require fixtures that have a standard, screw-in socket, just like a normal household bulb. A waterproof cord supplies electricity to the fixture, and enters through a waterproof seal. The only serviceable part inside the fixture is the light bulb. Fixtures and bulbs come in 120 or 240 volts; 120 volts are the most common for residential use. If the fixture becomes rusted or otherwise damaged, it cannot be fixed. The entire fixture has to be replaced.

Caution: *A light fixture is completely watertight and so the air inside of it becomes extremely hot. Without the cooling contact of water, the light will overheat. Never turn on a pool light unless there is water in the pool.*

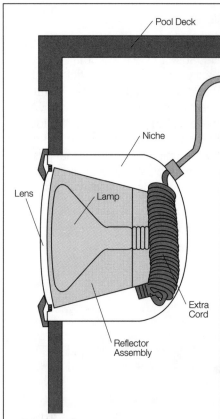

Lighting. A typical pool or spa light consists of a stainless steel, cone-shaped fixture, mounted in a watertight niche in the pool.

Replacing a Fixture

Fixtures come with attached, water-proof cords of 10 to 100 feet. Know the distance from the light niche to the junction box before you purchase a replacement fixture. Buy a longer cord than you think necessary and cut it to fit. As with all electrical repairs, turn off the power to the fixture at the circuit breaker and tape over it so no one turns it back on while you are working.

1 Disconnecting the Wiring. First locate the junction box. With many older pools, it is located in the deck directly above the light niche, under a 4-inch-diameter stainless steel or bronze cover plate (which is closed with three screws). Building codes presently require the junction box to be located at least 5 feet from the water and 18 inches above the surface of the water. When dealing with newer pools, check in the landscaping around the pool deck behind the niche.

Remove the junction box screws and take off the cover. Three wires enter the box from the switch and are connected to three that leave the box going to the light fixture. They are connected with wire connectors. The three wires going to the light fixture are colored black, white, and green (ground). They are individually insulated and bound together in a waterproof rubber sheath. Disconnect the three wires and unscrew the cord clamp that secures the cord to the junction box.

2 Removing the Old Fixture. Lean into the pool and unscrew the face-rim lock screw from the faceplate that holds the fixture in the niche. The top will float outward, but the bottom is hooked into the niche and must be lifted out. Uncoil the extra cord and allow the old fixture to float in the pool. Go back to the junction box and pull on the fixture cord. The fixture will move. Cords often swell from heat, age, or moisture, and may not budge. To lubricate a stubborn line, pour tile soap

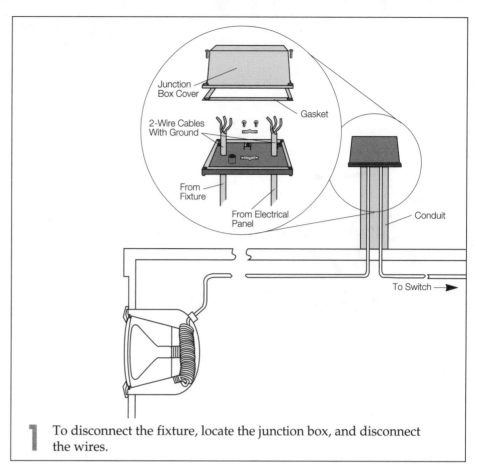

1 To disconnect the fixture, locate the junction box, and disconnect the wires.

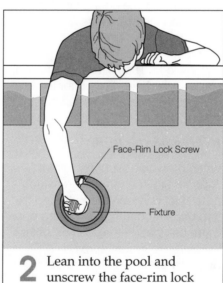

2 Lean into the pool and unscrew the face-rim lock screw holding the fixture.

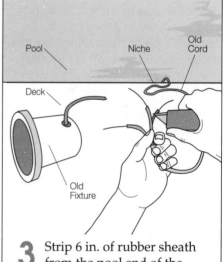

3 Strip 6 in. of rubber sheath from the pool end of the old cord.

from the junction box to the conduit. Allow the soap eight hours to slide all the way down the conduit.

3 Cutting off the Old Fixture. Use the old cord to pull new cord through the conduit from the niche to the junction box. Cut the old fixture from its cord. Strip 6 inches of

rubber sheath from the pool end of the old cord. Remove any paper threads and string that cover the wires in the cord.

4 Preparing the New Fixture. Be aware where you lay this delicate light—one kick and it will break. Take the cord from the new fixture

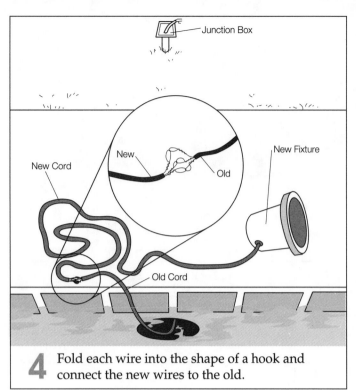

4 Fold each wire into the shape of a hook and connect the new wires to the old.

5 Pull the old cord from the junction box until the wire connection and the new cord emerge.

and strip back the sheath. Connect the new wires with the old by folding each wire into the shape of a hook. Connect the two hooks, and twist the loose ends around one another. Use electrical tape to tightly and thoroughly cover the exposed wire. Do not make the connection thicker than the cord, or it will not pass through the conduit. It must, however, be strong enough to hold the wires together.

5 Pulling the New Cord. Lay the new cord and fixture into the water. At the junction box, pull the old cord until the new connection and the new cord emerge. Keep pulling the cord until there is enough to reach from the fixture to the deck. This extra length of cord will be contained with the light fixture so that when the bulb has to be changed, the fixture can be pulled on deck. Untape the connection, and remove the old wires. At the junction, box end, cut off the excess wire so there is just enough to connect to the electrical supply lines in the junction box. Reconnect the wiring and close the junction box, reversing the procedure in Step 1, page 63.

6 Installing the New Fixture. Reach into the pool again, and

coil the excess cord around the fixture. Place the fixture in the niche, and replace the lock screw, reversing the procedure described in Step 2, page 63. If it is difficult to line up the face-rim lock screw and the hole in the niche, slide a coat hanger wire through the hole on the faceplate and into the screw hole on the niche. Then slide the fixture into place so the holes line up for the screw. Remove the coat hanger, and install the screw. Then test the light.

Replacing the Bulb

When replacing a bulb, it is most important to keep the fixture waterproof. Not only can the bulb and fixture become damaged, but the pool water can become electrified unless the circuit is protected by a GFCI. Begin by turning off the light at the circuit breaker, taping it in the "OFF" position. Then remove the fixture from the niche as previously described. (See "Replacing a Fixture," Step 2, page 63.) Lay the fixture on the pool deck.

1 Disassembling the Fixture. To remove the lens clamp, loosen the screws that hold it in place. Gently pry the lens from the fixture. Do not gouge the lens gasket.

6 If the light fixture does not line up with the niche, slide a wire coat hanger through the hole on the faceplate and into the screw hole of the niche.

2 Replacing the Bulb. Unscrew the old bulb, and screw in the new one. Some fixtures contain a bare-coiled spring wire. It is not wired to the electrical current and is designed to break the circuit. If the bulb breaks while in use, the spring sweeps across the filament, cutting the electricity in the circuit. This safety item ensures that if water does get into the fixture, the next swimmer does not get electrocuted.

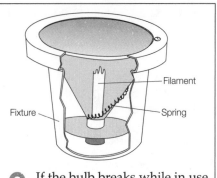

Clamp Lens Gasket

Fixture

1 Remove the lens clamp by loosening the screws.

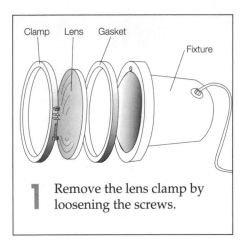

Filament

Fixture

Spring

2 If the bulb breaks while in use, the spring sweeps across the filament to break the circuit.

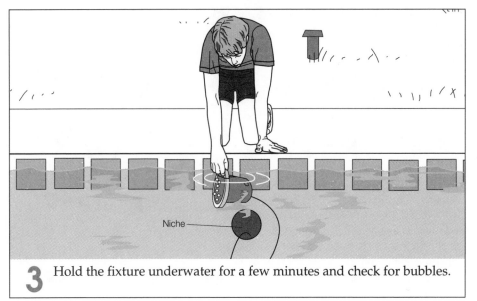

Niche

3 Hold the fixture underwater for a few minutes and check for bubbles.

Before reassembling the fixture, place it on the deck and briefly turn on the light to make sure it works. Normally a closed fixture is not turned on while out of the water. With the lens off, however, the heat can escape.

3 **Reassembling the Fixture.** To reassemble the fixture, simply reverse the procedure described in Steps 1 and 2. In addition, replace the gasket. An old gasket has been exposed to months of chemicals, heat, and compression. Place the new gasket around the lens as if it were a rubber band stretched around a drinking glass. If the faceplate screws into place, tighten the screws on opposite sides to apply even pressure on the gasket and avoid gaps which later cause leaks. Replace the fixture in the niche as described in "Replacing a Fixture,"

Step 6, page 64. Before doing so, however, hold the fixture underwater for a few minutes and check for bubbles (which indicate a leak). If there is a leak, again disassemble the fixture to reseat the gasket for a proper seal.

Covers

Pool and spa covers make sense financially, ecologically, and aesthetically. They help water retain warmth, keeping down the cost of heating. They slow down evaporation, which means less chemicals have to be added to the pool. They also prevent dirt and debris from entering the water, saving time in vacuuming and cleaning the filter.

Installing Bubble Solar Covers

The "bubble" (or sealed air) solar cover basically is a large sheet of bubble wrap—the same kind used for packaging. The cover has a bumpy side and a flat side. The sun warms the air in the bubbles, which in turn warms the water. The trapped air also keeps heat from escaping the water. Bubble covers are lightweight, flexible, thin, and easy to cut (use a razor knife or scissors). Bubble covers are sold in sheets from 5x5 feet for spas, to 30x50 feet for pools. They are inexpensive and last from two to four years, depending on wear and tear, weather, and water chemistry.

1 **Preparing the Cover.** Lay the cover on the water surface (bubble-side down) and leave it for two to three days. During this time it is okay to take it off to use the pool or spa. The waiting period allows the cover, which has been folded in a box, time to relax to its full size. Fur-

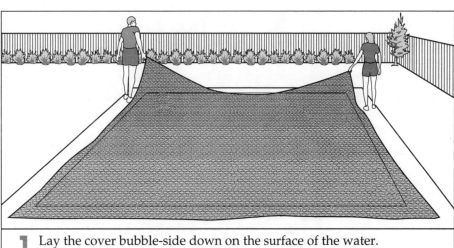

1 Lay the cover bubble-side down on the surface of the water.

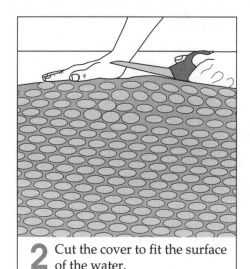

2 Cut the cover to fit the surface of the water.

thermore, cold water may cause the material to shrink about 5 percent, so the actual size of the cover is not fully realized until after this waiting period.

2 **Cutting the Cover to Size.** Use a razor knife, scissors, or shears to cut the cover to fit the water's surface. Always cut less rather than more. It is easy to go back and cut again, but there is no way to replace what has already been cut.

Other Types of Covers

Polypropylene. This type of cover is used during the winter to cover a pool or spa that is located in a cold climate. It is similar to the bubble cover, but it does not have bubbles. It does not insulate well, and it does not float. It is, however, an inexpensive way to cover a pool or spa. Ballast bags or sandbags are sold with polypropylene to anchor the cover on the deck.

Electric. This heavy, strong cover—made of sheet vinyl—is reinforced with thread or fabric and retracted on a roller that is operated by an electric motor. Electric covers often are concealed in a box bench or under one end of the deck. The cover material is stretched between tracks or rollers found around the edge of the pool coping; a motor-driven pulley system rolls it around a barrel roller. The companies that manufacture electric covers sell and service them, so it is best to let a professional install and repair yours.

Mesh. Made of a close-woven mesh, this cover is designed for security. This type of cover ensures that no one will fall into the water. The mesh is similar to the strips used on lawn chairs, but it is reinforced with steel or other wires that crisscross the fabric. Like reinforced vinyl covers, mesh covers are installed with hooks and

A roller (or reel) system eases the handling of a bubble cover, which otherwise might require lifting, folding, cutting it into two pieces, or finding a place to put it. The cover is attached with straps to the barrel of the roller. When the barrel is rotated the straps roll up first and then reel in the rest of the cover until it is wrapped neatly around the barrel.

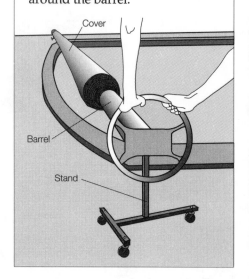

eyes on the cover and the deck. The cover doesn't touch the water. It lets rain through but not leaves and the like.

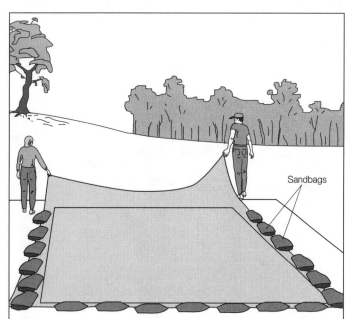

Polypropylene. Ballast bags or sandbags are used to anchor the plastic cover to the deck.

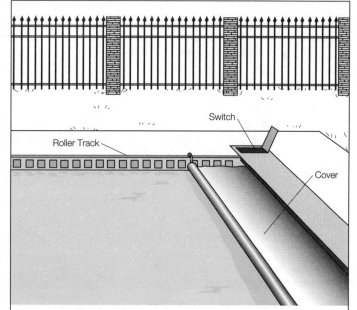

Electric. The cover is stretched between tracks or rollers found on the edge of the pool coping.

WINTERIZING A POOL OR SPA

If you live in a climate that experiences four distinct seasons, there are certain measures that must be taken to protect your pool during the colder months. Even if you live in a warmer climate, some winterizing tips can be useful.

Closing a Pool

The long winter months bring many dangers to pools and spas. Freezing water trapped inside pipes and equipment expands and can be damaging. PVC plastic pipes, plumbing fittings, soft copper heat exchangers, and even galvanized pipes are susceptible. In addition, still water promotes algae growth (which blossoms in the spring); and heavy rain introduces leaves and debris which clog the system and cause stains.

These problems, among others, are good reasons to properly prepare a pool for the winter. In most cases, the pool will be shut down completely. The circulation system is drained entirely, with the lines blown out by air from a compressor or air pump and plugged. Aboveground pools and spas have to be drained completely. Inground plastic or gunite spas are treated like pools.

1 **Winterizing the Water Chemistry.** To prevent scaling and etching, properly adjust the pH before closing the pool. To prevent algae and staining, shock the pool (use triple the amount of chlorine normally used for shocking; see page 16). Raise the chlorine residual to 30 parts per million for plaster pools;10 parts per million for vinyl or plastic. Add a chelating agent so metals do not stain the surface. Add an algicide to inhibit black algae growth. Chelating agents and algicides are strong chemicals, so follow the label instructions.

Since it is important to circulate these products thoroughly before shutting down the system, the products will have to be added based on the volume of the pool (in gallons) even though the pool will be partially emptied for the winter. When winterizing a pool, use liquids or powders, rather than tablets or floaters, to dispense the chemicals. Without circulation, a tablet will dissolve in one area, damaging or staining the pool (especially vinyl or plastic surfaces). Make sure that all of the added chemicals have a

1 Before shutting down the system for the winter, make sure the chemicals have a chance to circulate adequately.

2 Completely clean the pool. Dirt and debris left in the water for a long period of stagnation create stains.

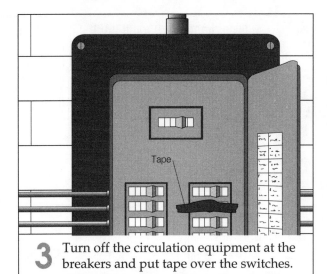

3 Turn off the circulation equipment at the breakers and put tape over the switches.

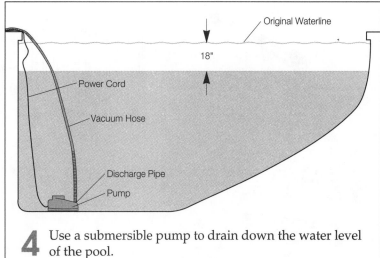

4 Use a submersible pump to drain down the water level of the pool.

chance to circulate adequately before shutting down the system.

2 **Cleaning the Pool.** Use a leaf rake and then a vacuum to thoroughly clean the pool (see chapter 6, page 49). Dirt and debris left in the water for a long period of stagnation leave stubborn stains that are difficult to remove in the spring.

3 **Shutting Down the Electrical Equipment.** Turn off the circulation equipment at the breakers, and put tape over the switches so they are not turned on until spring. Turn off all manual switches and time clocks. Remove the trippers on time clocks just in case the breaker is turned on accidentally.

4 **Draining the Pool.** One of the main reasons for winterizing the pool is to protect the equipment and plumbing from damages caused by freezing water. Use a submersible pump to drain the water to a level 18 inches below the skimmer. Attach a vacuum hose to the discharge pipe of the pump and run the hose to a waste drain or sewer line. Submersible pumps are fairly inexpensive, but they can usually be rented at tool rental stores. If your equipment permits, the water level can be lowered by vacuuming to the discharge port of the filter during the last cleanup. This accomplishes two tasks at once.

Caution: *Do not drain all the water*

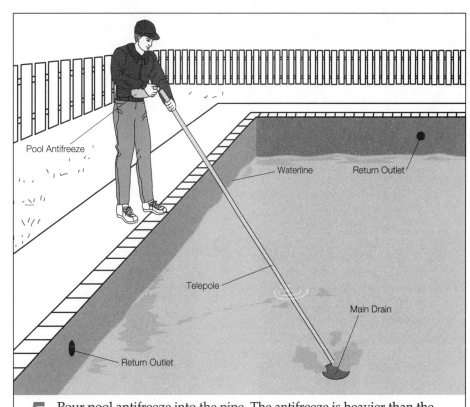

5 Pour pool antifreeze into the pipe. The antifreeze is heavier than the water and will flow into the main drain plumbing.

out of the pool (or in-ground spa) because hydrostatic pressure can cause cracks, or worse, it can cause the whole pool to pop out of the ground. Vinyl pools sometimes ripple when left empty for the winter, and the folds in the vinyl can stretch and weaken the material.

5 **Winterizing the Circulation Plumbing.** After draining, there are three options to winterizing the

plumbing. The easiest method is to simply empty all the water in the lines by running the pump. Since the water is below the level of the return lines, the water will empty out. Do not continue to run the pump once the plumbing is empty.

Filling the plumbing with pool antifreeze is the second option to winterizing. Insert a hollow telepole into the pool and hold one end over

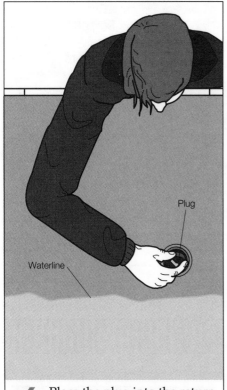

6 Place the plug into the return outlet and tighten the wing nut so it expands to fill the space.

7 Use a coating of petroleum jelly to protect exposed metal fixtures from corrosion.

Plug

Waterline

Petroleum Jelly

Waterline

the main drain. Pour pool antifreeze into the pipe. Since the antifreeze is heavier than the water, it will flow into the main drain plumbing. Using a wet/dry vacuum, suck as much water as you can out of the pipes, the pump strainer pot, and the suction line that feeds it. Then pour pool antifreeze into the pipes via the strainer pot and allow it to flow back into the pool. If there is a check valve in the pipe, water will not flow all the way back into the pool (add as much antifreeze as the line will take).

The third method to winterizing the plumbing is to add antifreeze before draining any water at all. For this method, start the pump with the strainer pot lid open. While the pump is running, pour the antifreeze into the pump. The antifreeze can be colored with food dye to make it more visible. After the antifreeze has travelled through the system, it will be visible from the return ports. When you see antifreeze coming out, plug the return lines and then quickly turn off the pump. Drain the water to the

level of 18 inches below the skimmer and tile line.

6 **Plugging the Return Lines.** Immediately after the water has left the plumbing lines, or they have been filled with pool antifreeze, it's time to plug them. Unscrew the collar or nozzle fittings of the return lines. (You won't find these on a gunite pool.) If they are tight use adjustable pliers to unscrew them. Remove any eyeballs (the round ball with the hole in it that directs the stream of water out of the fitting) from the return lines. Then plug them with expandable rubber plugs. Most pool and spa returns lines are 1 inch in diameter, so buy plugs that expand to that size. If in doubt, unscrew one collar and eyeball and take it to a pool supply store so they can provide the proper plug. The plugs are easy to use. Just insert them in the return outlet and tighten the wing nut. The plug expands to fill the space.

7 **Securing the Deck.** Remove and store pool equipment that

can be damaged by the weather. This includes deck furniture, the diving board, safety equipment, rails, ladders, and anything else that weathers poorly. If the rails, metal ladders, and light fixtures cannot be removed, coat them with a layer of petroleum jelly to protect them from corrosion. Close off access to the pool and lock all gates. Store all hoses as straight as possible or coiled in large loops.

Securing Pool Supplies

Since they lose their potency, chemicals and test kit reagents that will not be used over the winter months can be properly disposed. Acids and soda ash are the only products that persevere until spring. Make sure they are placed in watertight containers and stored in a well-ventilated area.

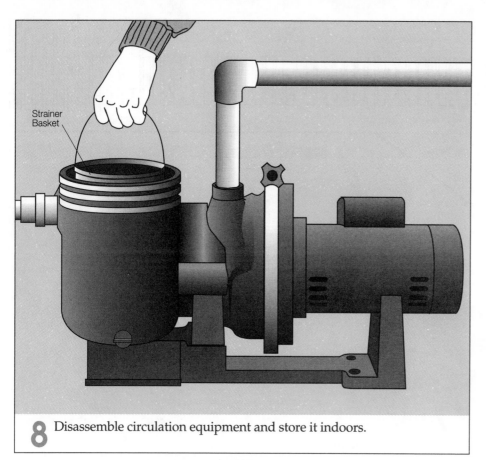

8 Disassemble circulation equipment and store it indoors.

9 Put some gravel in an empty plastic bottle and place it in the skimmer.

8 **Securing the Circulation Equipment.** Disassemble this equipment and store it indoors. Except for gunite pools, remove the pump and motor unit. (See chapter 3, page 23.) If the plumbing makes pump removal difficult, unbolt the motor from the volute and remove it. After disconnecting the motor wiring, use electrical tape to tape the wire ends of the pump. This step is taken as a safety precaution in the unlikely event that the power is turned back on before the equipment is reinstalled.

Disassemble, clean, and drain the filter thoroughly. (See chapter 4, page 33.) Put the grids and cartridges in storage. Freezing can deteriorate the fabric. Clean and drain sand filters. Close the filter tank so rain and debris do not fill it.

Close the gas valve to the heater and the supply valve (if it is exclusively for the heater) at the meter. The heater has drain plugs. Open them, and drain the heater.

Remove and store spa jet or automatic cleaner booster pumps. Drain the automatic cleaner plumbing, or fill it with antifreeze. The nice thing about the automatic cleaner is that the plumbing outlet will be above the waterline, making draining and plugging easy.

9 **Taking Extra Precautions.** Put three to four inches of gravel in an empty plastic bottle, and place it in the skimmer. The gravel helps the bottle remain upright in the skimmer should it become filled with rain or snow. If the water freezes, the ice will compress the bottle rather than crack the skimmer. Fill two or three plastic jugs about one quarter of the way with water, and leave them floating in the pool. If the water in the pool freezes, the ice will crush the jugs rather than the walls of the pool or spa.

10 **Covering the Pool.** Any type of cover is better than no cover at all. Polypropylene covers are inexpensive and can be held in place with sandbags placed around the

10 Sheet vinyl covers are inexpensive and can be held in place with sandbags.

Labels on image: Sandbags, Vinyl Cover

edge of the pool. If your pool cover is mesh for water security, cover it with an additional layer of polypropylene; the mesh does not keep out dirt and sunlight.

Temperate Climates

Those who live in a part of the country that is temperate need to keep an eye on weather reports to prevent getting surprised by freezing temperatures. During a cold snap, run the circulation system 24 hours a day with the heater set on the lowest setting.

Those who are not going to be home, and yet expect it to be cold, are advised to set the time clock to run two hours during the day, two hours late in the evening, and two hours in the early morning. Doing so prevents the water from freezing.

Reopening the Pool

The reopening process begins the moment the pool is closed. By keeping an eye on the pool over the winter, the reopening process becomes that much easier. Snow or rain can raise the water level or sink the cover. Since heavy debris can fall in, it is better to remove it immediately than in the spring. Reopening the pool entails reversing the instructions for closing it. Review the previous procedures; the following is a handy checklist:

■ **Supplies.** Take the supplies out of storage and replace those that have exceeded the expiration date.

■ **Uncover.** Remove the cover, and then scrub and rinse it. Allow it to dry (to prevent mildew) before folding and storing it for the summer.

■ **Equipment.** Reinstall or reassemble the pump, filter, and other removed items.

■ **Deck.** Reinstall ladders, diving board, and other deck fittings. Most of the petroleum jelly used to coat exposed metal fittings will have weathered off. Use a dry terry cloth towel to wipe off the remainder.

■ **Plumbing.** Remove the plugs and replace return outlet fittings.

■ **Refilling the Pool.** Bring the water level up to normal.

■ **Electrical.** Restore circuit breakers, switches, and time clock trippers to normal operating positions.

■ **Cleaning.** Restart the circulation equipment and clean the pool.

■ **Chemistry.** Balance the water chemistry and check the levels frequently during the first few days (until they stabilize). The antifreeze decomposes, losing most of its potency over the winter. The remainder will be diluted by the addition of fresh water. If you add house water that is normally softened, turn off the softener.

Run the circulation system 24 hours straight for three days or until the water has cleared completely. Depending on how dirty the pool became over the winter, the filter must be cleaned once or twice during this period.

SPAS & HOT TUBS

Like a pool, a spa is a large container of heated, filtered, circulating water. There are, however, some pieces of equipment used for a spa that are not used for a swimming pool. Spas and hot tubs differ from pools primarily in that they use air blowers to create the swirling water. The equipment used for circulating the water in a spa or hot tub is smaller than that used for a pool and often is built into an integrated unit. In addition, spas and hot tubs require more stringent chemical demands.

Spa Equipment

The biggest difference between pool and spa equipment is that spas usually incorporate air blowers to create the bubbling turbulence that makes them so enjoyable. Spa pumps and motors are the same as those used for pools, but many spas use two pumps. One pump serves the circulation system, while the other provides maximum power to the jets. Gas heaters that are used for spas are generally small versions of pool heaters; electric heaters are used for portable spas. Finally, spas usually have cartridge filters instead of the larger DE or sand filters used for pools. Portable spas often combine all the support equipment into a combination unit called a "skid pack."

Replacing an Air Blower

It is important to use the right sized blower for your particular spa. If the blower is too large, it forces more air through the system than the lines can handle, causing the motor to overheat and eventually burn out. If the blower is too small, the flow of air that passes through the system is either weak or nonexistent.

Most blower failure is caused by interference within the system which causes the blower motor to overheat. Before replacing a fairly new blower, check for obstructions that block the pathway of air. There are no serviceable parts inside the blower, so if the blower continues to fail, replace it. Blowers must be compatible with the circulation system and plumbing. Make sure one blower is replaced with another of the same size.

Caution: As always, begin by turning off the electrical supply at the circuit breaker panel and tape the breaker to be sure no one accidentally turns it back on while you are working.

1 Disconnecting the Old Blower. The electrical wiring for the blower is located in a junction box that is attached to the blower housing. To expose the wires, unscrew the two screws that hold the cover of the junction box. Inside, there is an electrical 120-volt "hot" line and a neutral line (if the blower is a 120-volt unit); or two hot lines of 120 volts (if the unit is a 240-volt unit). Remove the wire connectors to disconnect the wires. Unscrew the conduit from the

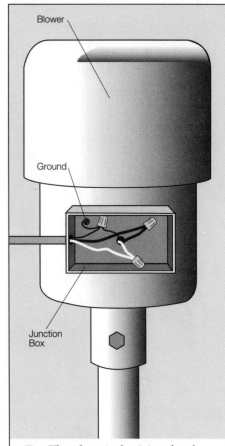

1 The electrical wiring for the blower is housed in a junction box which is attached to the blower housing.

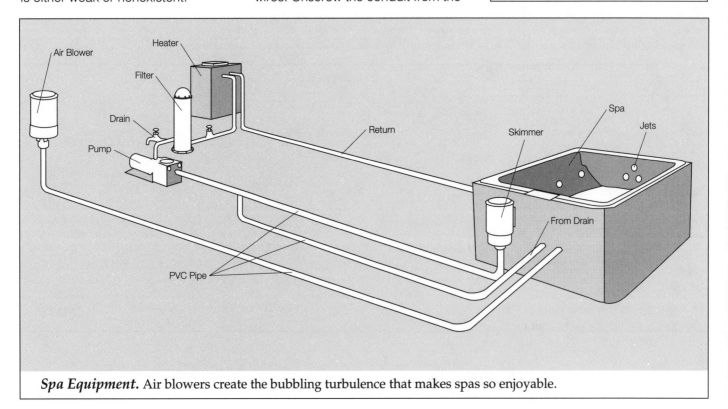

Spa Equipment. Air blowers create the bubbling turbulence that makes spas so enjoyable.

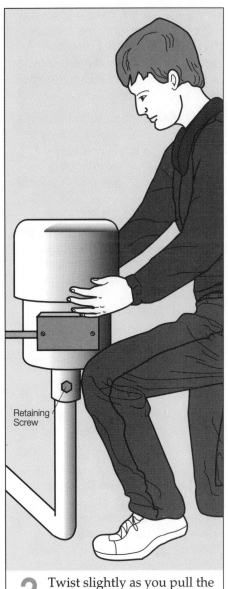

Retaining Screw

2 Twist slightly as you pull the blower away from the pipe.

junction box and pull the wiring away from the blower.

2 **Removing the Old Blower.**
Loosen the retaining screw located below the blower. Twist the blower slightly as it is pulled away from the pipe. The blower itself lifts off the air pipe. Most blowers are not glued to the air pipe, but if yours is, use a hacksaw to cut the air pipe just below the blower.

3 **Installing the New Blower.** Set the new blower on the air pipe, pushing it on as far as it will go. Tighten the retaining screw and re-connect the conduit and wiring by reversing Step 1.

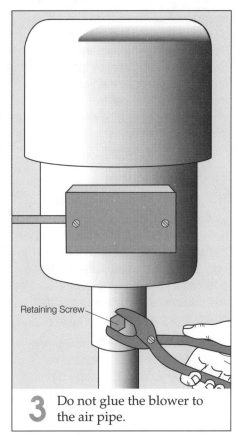

Retaining Screw

3 Do not glue the blower to the air pipe.

Using a Booster Pump

Some spas use the circulating pump (the main pump) to power the jets. Other spas add a second booster pump to increase water turbulence. (Both types use air blowers to create turbulence.) A booster pump is identical to the circulating pump.

Just like the circulation pump, the booster pump requires a strainer basket. The circulation pump is connected to the skimmer, and its basket traps large bits of debris, such as leaves. The booster strainer basket traps smaller debris, such as hair and grit.

Small spas use a two-speed motor on one pump instead of two separate pumps. The low speed is used for heating and circulating, while the high speed is used for boosting the power to the jets. The service and repair of booster pumps is the same as described in the chapter on pumps and motors. (See page 23.)

Electric Heaters

Larger spas use gas heaters, while smaller ones use electric heaters. (See page 43.) Electric heaters. also are used when gas service is not available and in places where venting is not possible. (Gas heaters require extensive ventilation.) It takes electric heaters longer to heat the water than it does gas heaters. For this reason, it is a good idea to help retain the heat by covering the spa.

Skid Packs

A skid pack is a complete spa circulation system mounted on a metal

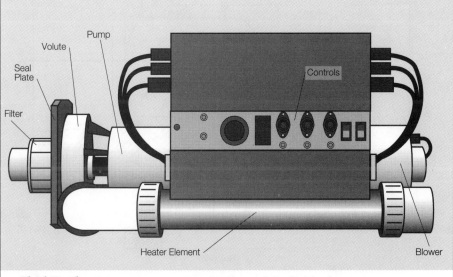

Seal Plate · Volute · Pump · Filter · Controls · Heater Element · Blower

Skid Packs. It is necessary to maintain each individual component—pump, filter, controls—in a skid pack.

frame called a skid. These units come preplumbed and eliminate the need to choose and match components. Skid packs often are found on compact installations, such as portable spas. A skid pack usually is comprised of a pump, two-speed motor, heater, control devices, blower, and filter.

Maintaining a skid pack means maintaining each individual component. The only difference is that a number of components may have to be disassembled in order to get at the one that needs repair.

For skid packs, control system failure is a fairly common problem. The control system is made up of switches, thermostat controls, a time clock, high and low speed pump controls, and lights. Some skid packs have a plug-in circuit board where components plug into individual outlets. The switching system controls the

electrical flow to each outlet. When a blower fails to operate, unplug it from the switching system controls, and use a multimeter to test the outlet. No current means the switch, the wiring, or the control circuit is the problem—not the blower. If a current is present, the blower is at fault and needs to be replaced.

Three-Port Valves

The three-port valve often is used when a pool and spa share one filter, heater, and pump. In this situation, the water is alternately diverted to the pool or spa. Spas also use the three-port valve to divert air bubbles and jet water to one side of the spa or the other, or a combination of both.

Shaped like the letter Y or T, three-port valves are designed to take water flow coming from one direction and divide it into a choice of two other directions (or a combina-

tion of the two). A handle placed on top of the valve turns the diverter 180 degrees in either direction, directing the flow and mixture of water that passes through the spa's circulation system.

Lubrication is the most important measure to take when it comes to maintaining a three-port valve. A valve that becomes difficult to turn places stress on the shaft. Lubricate the valve every six months or when valve operation feels stiff. This twice-a-year ritual is important, especially for motorized valves, because the motor will strain against old, sticky gaskets until the diverter and shaft break, or the motor burns out completely. Use only pure silicone lubricant to lubricate the gasket. Most other lubricants are petroleum-based and can dissolve the gaskets.

1 Disassembling the Valve. Unscrew the handle screws and pull the handle off of the shaft. Unscrew the cover screws and lift off the cover. Pull the diverter out of the valve body.

2 Lubricating the Diverter. If the diverter or stem is broken, replace it with a one-piece unit. If the seal gasket looks old, use needle-nose pliers to pull it away from the diverter. Use your finger to apply silicone lubricant liberally to the diverter and the new gasket, and then reassemble.

3 Reassembling and Testing. Gently twist the diverter as it is inserted into the valve body. Rotate the diverter back and forth (180 degrees) several times to be sure enough silicone lubricant has been applied before screwing the cap in place.

Leaks in Three-Port Valves

Common problems with three-port valves are leaks. If the valve leaks from under the cover, either the cover gasket needs to be replaced or the cover is loose. Sheet-metal screws attach the cover to the valve body, and if tightened too much,

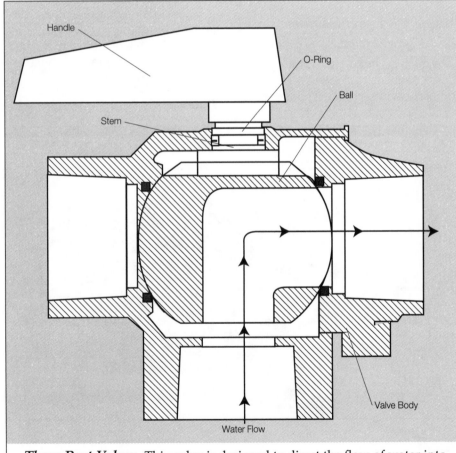

Three-Port Valves. This valve is designed to direct the flow of water into two directions.

they strip out the holes and no longer work. In that case, a screw slightly longer or wider is needed to grip the plastic again. Be sure to use stainless steel so the screw does not rust or break down and cause a leak. If larger screws already were used, and there is not enough plastic left on the body to grip, the entire valve must be replaced. Using PVC glue or fiberglass resin to fill a screw hole is only a temporary repair.

Leaks also can occur inside the valve, causing water to slip past the diverter seal to the closed side of the valve. Meanwhile, the water is not totally diverted in the intended direction. If the spa drains or overflows for no reason, it could be that the diverter is not precisely aligned toward the intended port. Follow the steps outlined for lubrication and gasket replacement to solve this common problem. If the diverter gasket becomes worn or excessively compressed, it cannot stop water from getting past. Check the gasket and if there is even the slightest amount of damage, replace it. It does not take much compression to cause bypass leaks.

Bypass leaks also result when the diverter itself has shrunk or warped. This sometimes happens when the spa water is very hot or the system ran dry and overheated. Such shrinkage is difficult to see, and does not have to be extensive to cause a bypass leak.

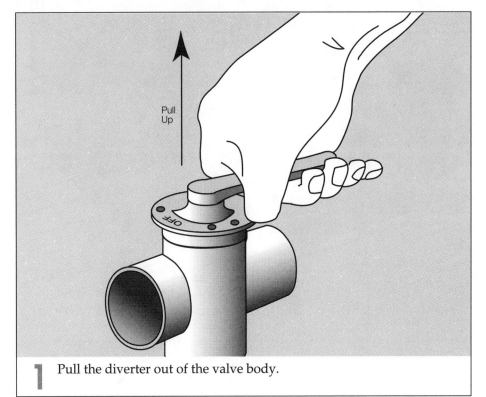

1 Pull the diverter out of the valve body.

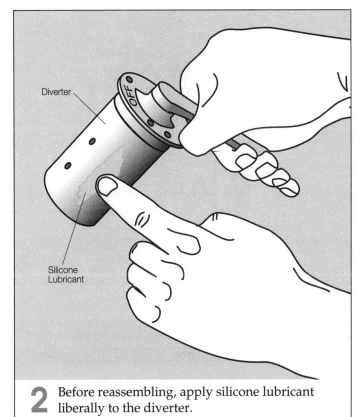

2 Before reassembling, apply silicone lubricant liberally to the diverter.

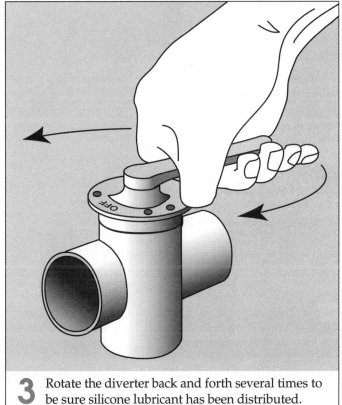

3 Rotate the diverter back and forth several times to be sure silicone lubricant has been distributed.

Covering the Spa

Because they are much smaller and easier to cover than pools, there are a wide variety of spa covers from which to choose. Covers retain water heat, keep out dirt and debris, and ensure safety.

Wood. Sturdy and easy to lock, a wood cover is an effective way to keep children out of a spa while reaping all the benefits of a cover. Many wooden covers are made with two sections that can be hinged for convenience or left separate. Use only stainless steel or bronze nails and screws, as well as rot-resistant woods such as cedar, redwood, and red oak. Pine and fir rot quickly unless pressure-treated and varnished, making them more expensive than simply using a better timber. Never paint a wooden cover; the heat and chemicals peel paint rapidly.

Reinforced Upholstered Foam. These covers are made from foam that is framed with plastic or aluminum and covered with fabric or plastic. They are a popular alternative to wood covers. Often this type of cover consists of two sections that are connected with a fabric hinge. Foam covers are significantly lighter than wood covers and more expensive as well.

Wood and Foam. This popular cover, a variation on the reinforced upholstered foam, consists partially of redwood slats. The foam connects the slats and provides insulation, while the slats provide rigid safety without the weight of a solid-wood cover. In addition, it can be rolled up for removal and storage.

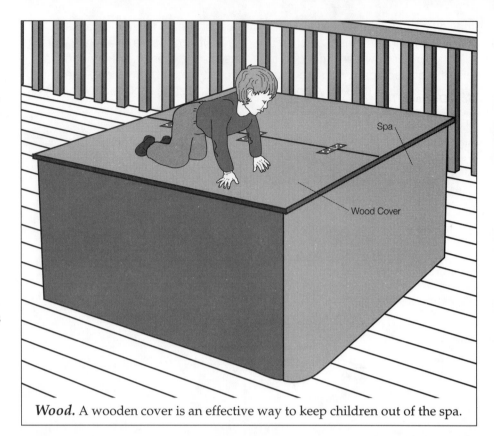

Wood. A wooden cover is an effective way to keep children out of the spa.

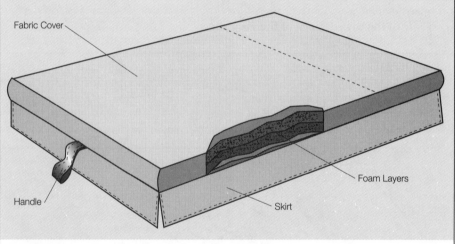

Reinforced Upholstered Foam. This cover is made of foam that is framed with plastic or aluminum and covered with fabric.

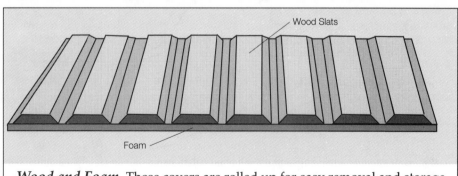

Wood and Foam. These covers are rolled up for easy removal and storage.

Acid Demand The amount of acid required by a body of water to raise the pH to neutral (7).

Algicides Chemical substances that kill algae or inhibit their growth in water.

Alkalinity The characteristic of water that registers a pH above neutral (7).

Automatic Gas Valve The valve that controls the release of natural or propane gas to a heater. Also called a "combination gas valve."

Backwash Process of running water through a filter opposite the normal direction of flow to flush out contaminants.

Balance The term used in water chemistry to indicate that when measuring all components together, the water is neither scaling nor corrosive.

Blow Bag A device attached to a garden hose with an outlet that expands to create a seal and force the water into an opening.

Blower An electromechanical device that generates air pressure to provide spa jets and rings with bubbles.

Bridging The condition existing when DE and dirt closes the intended gaps between filter grids in a DE filter.

Channeling Creation of a tube or "channel" in a sand filter through which water will flow unfiltered.

Check Valve A valve that permits flow of water or air in only one direction through a pipe.

Chelating Agent Chemical compounds which prevent minerals in solution in a body of water from precipitating out of solution and depositing on surfaces.

Chloramine Compound of chlorine when combined with inorganic ammonia or nitrogen. Chloramines are stable and slow to release their chlorine for oxidizing (sanitizing) purposes.

Chlorine A substance used to sanitize water by oxidizing (killing) bacteria; generally available in liquid, solid (tablets or sticks), and granular form.

Chlorine Demand The amount of chlorine required (demanded) by a body of water to raise the chlorine residual to a level that sanitizes the water.

Chlorine, Free Available That portion of chlorine in a body of water that is immediately capable (available) of oxidizing contaminants.

Chlorine Residual The amount of chlorine remaining in a body of water after all organic material (including bacteria) has been oxidized. Expressed in parts per million. The total chlorine residual is the sum of all free available chlorine plus any combined chlorine (chloramine).

Diatomaceous Earth (DE) A white, powdery substance composed of tiny prehistoric skeletal remains of algae (diatoms), used as a water filtration media in DE filters.

Diverter Plastic or bronze adapter pipe that fits into a skimmer port to facilitate connection of a vacuum hose. The diverter can divert all suction to the skimmer, closing off the main drain or vice versa.

Etching Corrosion of a surface by water that is acidic or low in total alkalinity or hardness.

Floater A chemical feeder system whereby a sanitizer tablet is placed in the device and it is allowed to float and dissolve in the body of water.

Free Chlorine Also called "available chlorine." Chlorine in its elemental form, not combined with other elements, available for sanitization of water.

Fusible Link A safety device in the control circuit located near the burner tray of a heater. If the link detects heat in excess of a preset limit, it melts and breaks the circuit to shut off the heater.

Gallons Per Minute (GPM) A unit of measurement for liquids.

Hardness Also called "calcium hardness." The amount of dissolved minerals (mostly calcium and magnesium) in a body of water. In unbalanced water, high levels cause scale and low levels corrode surfaces and equipment.

High Limit Switch A safety device used in the control circuit of heaters. When the high limit switch detects temperatures in excess of its preset maximum, it breaks the control circuit to shut down the heater.

Intermittent Ignition Device (IID) The electronic control and switching device used in electronic ignition heaters to operate the control circuit and automatic gas valve.

Laterals The horizontal filter grids at the bottom of a sand filter.

Multiport Valve A valve having at least four positions to direct water flow.

Neutral The pH reading at which the substance being measured is neither acidic nor alkaline. Neutral pH is 7.0.

O-Ring Thin rubber gasket used to create a waterproof seal in certain plumbing joints or between two parts of a device, such as between the lid and the strainer pot on a pump.

Parts Per Million (PPM) A measurement of the concentration of a substance in a liquid. For example, 3 ppm equals 3 pounds of a substance for a million pounds of a liquid.

Potential Hydrogen (pH) The relative acidity or alkalinity of soil or water, expressed on a scale of 0–14 where 7 is neutral, 0 is extremely acidic, 14 extremely alkaline. Pool water must be between 7.2 and 7.8 pH.

Prime The process of initiating water flow in a pump to commence circulation by displacing air in the suction side of the circulation system.

Pumice A natural soft, abrasive stone substance (similar to lava rock) used to clean pool tiles.

Reagent A liquid or dry chemical that has been formulated for water testing. A substance that reacts to another known substance, producing a predictable color in the water.

Residual The amount of a substance remaining in a body of water after the demand for that substance has been met.

Sanitizer Any chemical compound that oxidizes organic material and bacteria to provide a clean water environment.

Scale Calcium carbonate deposits that form on pool surfaces.

Shaft Extender A bronze fitting added to the shaft of a motor to lengthen the shaft to accommodate the design of the pump being used.

Shocking See "Superchlorination."

Skimmer A part of the circulation system that removes debris from the surface of the water.

Slurry A thin mixture of DE and water.

Soda Ash (sodium carbonate) A white powdery substance used to raise the pH of water.

Superchlorination Periodic application of extremely high levels of chlorine (in excess of 3 ppm) to completely oxidize any organic material in a body of water and leave a substantial chlorine residual. Also called "shocking."

Three-Port Valve A plumbing fitting used to divert flow from one direction into two other directions.

Total Alkalinity The measurement of all alkaline substances (carbonates, bicarbonates, and hydroxides) in water.

Union Plumbing fitting connecting two pipes by means of threaded male and female counterparts on the ends of pipes.

Weir The barrier in a skimmer over which water flows. A floating weir raises and lowers its level to match the water level in a pool or spa.